# On Wings of Joy

# On Wings of Joy

## The Story of Ballet
## from the 16th Century to Today

Written by Trudy Garfunkel

**Little, Brown and Company**
Boston   New York   London   Toronto

First Edition

Illustration credits:
Pages 54, 81, 120, 143, 159, and 162: Costas. Page 132: Louis Péres. Page 151: Photograph by Maurice Seymour, courtesy of Ronald Seymour. Page 165: ©1993 Martha Swope. Page 178: Dance Collection, the New York Public Library for the Performing Arts; Astor, Lenox, and Tilden Foundations; courtesy of the School of American Ballet. All other illustrations are courtesy of the Dance Collection, the New York Public Library for the Performing Arts; Astor, Lenox, and Tilden Foundations.

"between green/ mountains" is reprinted from *Complete Poems, 1913–1962*, by e. e. cummings, by permission of Liveright Publishing Corporation. Copyright 1923, 1925, 1931, 1935, 1938, 1939, 1940, 1944, 1945, 1946, 1947, 1948, 1949, 1950, 1951, 1952, 1953, 1954, 1955, 1956, 1957, 1958, 1959, 1960, 1961, 1962 by the Trustees for the E. E. Cummings Trust. Copyright © 1961, 1963, 1968 by Marion Morehouse Cummings.

The epigraph at page 180 is reprinted by permission of Harold Ober Associates Incorporated. Copyright © 1962, 1990 by Agnes de Mille.

Library of Congress Cataloging-in-Publication Data

Garfunkel, Trudy.
On wings of joy : the story of ballet from the 16th century to today / written by Trudy Garfunkel : — 1st ed.
p.    cm.
Includes bibliographical references and index.
ISBN 0-316-30412-3
1. Ballet — History — Juvenile literature. [1. Ballet — History.]
I. Title.
GV1787.6.G37        1994
792.8'09 — dc20

93-41526

10 9 8 7 6 5 4 3 2 1

FG

Published simultaneously in Canada
by Little, Brown & Company (Canada) Limited

Printed in the United States of America

To my parents

And to dancers — past and
present — who bring so much joy
with their art

*Acknowledgments*

*The Dance Collection of the New York Public Library is an invaluable research resource; I would like to thank the librarians and staff for their help.*

*And my special appreciation to Leslie and Richard Curtis for their continuing support and encouragement.*

On with the dance! Let joy be unconfined.

— Lord Byron
From "Childe Harold"

# Contents

# Prologue

allet is a universe of the imagination, a place of magic and enchantment, beauty and romance. Its many worlds vibrate with graceful dancers, glorious music, and sumptuous costumes. There are ballets that can make you cry, make you laugh, or send shivers up and down your spine. There are others that celebrate the pure joy of movement and the streamlined energy and excitement of contemporary life. In the universe of ballet dwell Swan Queens and Fauns, Don Quixote and the Sleeping Beauty. You can travel from a village fair in old Russia to a rodeo in the American West, from a fantastic toy shop where dolls come to life to a mysterious forest radiant with magic and moonbeams. Whether a ballet is old or new, however, it reflects a tradition that began more than four hundred years ago in Europe. Today's classical ballet dancers learn steps descended from the social dances of Renaissance lords and ladies, and the art's elegant style harks back to the aristocratic manners practiced at Versailles by the courtiers of Louis XIV, the Sun King.

Ballet is sight, sound, and motion, the theatrical form that can tell a story without words or convey moods and emotions through music and movement. *On Wings of Joy* will introduce you to its fascinating history: how it began, how the technical innovations and stylistic changes evolved, and what it is like today. You will learn about the basic positions and movements of ballet, about toe shoes and tutus, about contemporary dance companies and legendary ones that no longer exist. You will meet ballet superstars of the past and present, great choreographers and the ballets they created — many of the people and events that have gone into making ballet the wondrous art that it is.

# Part I
# The Origins of Ballet

The entry of the Four Virtues — Faith, Justice, Charity, and Prudence — from the *Ballet Comique de la Reine* (1581). The Virtues wear elaborate star-studded costumes and carry symbolic emblems.

Shake off your heavy trance!
  And leap into a dance
Such as no mortals use to tread:
  Fit only for Apollo
To play to, for the moon to lead,
  And all the stars to follow!

— Francis Beaumont
From "The Masque of the Inner Temple"

# Overture

Dance may be the oldest art form. Drawings found on the walls of prehistoric caves show masked dancers imitating the movements of animals, possibly in the hope of taking on their strength or ensuring the success of the hunt. From very early times, dance has been used as a means of communication—to tell stories and to entertain. It has also been considered to possess religious and magical properties. Primitive societies have often used dancing to celebrate the harvest or in rituals surrounding birth and death.

The ancient Greeks used dance in their complex ceremonies and religious rites, because they believed that dancing brought the mind and body into perfect harmony. The festivals honoring the Greek god of wine, Dionysus, featured wild and spirited dancing, as did the plays that were presented at the foot of the Acropolis during these annual spring rites. Originally these dramas were performed by a chorus, dancers who sang, chanted, and moved in rhythmic patterns; later, playwrights added first one, then several actors to respond to the chorus and act out dramatic episodes.

The stage for the plays was known as the orchestra, or "dancing place," a large, flat circular area that was a feature of Greek theaters. Although only men could be actors and members of the chorus, the patron of dance, the Muse Terpsichore, was a goddess. She was one of nine sisters, all daughters of Zeus, each of whom presided over a different art or science.

Across Europe in the Middle Ages (c. A.D. 500–1300), the Catholic Church associated dance with pagan rituals and considered it the work of the devil. The church did not use it as part of its religious services. People at that time, however, used village festivals, such as May Day or weddings, as occasions for celebratory dancing, and communal dancing was often used for courtship as well.

During the Renaissance (c. A.D. 1300–1600), culture and the arts — including dance — flourished throughout Europe. For the entertainment of the common folk, traveling pageants, featuring singers and dancers, went from town to town in highly decorated carts or floats. But it was the lavish theatrical entertainments and courtly dance forms viewed and practiced by the aristocracy during this era that were to provide the first glimmers of what would later become ballet.

At court banquets, the nobility was entertained by disguised players and dancers called mummers. By the end of the fifteenth century, these feasts often included a series of interludes called *entrées*, or entries — dancing, singing, poetry, pantomime, and special mechanical effects presented between the courses of the meal. Special effects included clouds that descended from the heavens and changed color; revolving stages created scene changes. The singers and dancers were usually costumed as the gods and goddesses of Greek and Roman mythology.

In 1489, such a series of *entrées*, based on scenes from classical mythology, was prepared in honor of the marriage of Isabella of Aragon and the duke of Milan. At the wedding banquet, each dish was accompanied by appropriately costumed performers. Players portrayed Jason and the Argonauts capturing the Golden Fleece as the roast lamb was served, and dancers dressed as sea gods performed for the fish course.

Participatory dancing was also a significant part of the social life of the courts and noble houses of Europe during the Renaissance. Many nobles employed their own dancing masters, who were also expected to set the standards for etiquette and deportment. The ability to dance was an important part of an aristocrat's repertoire of

Court dancing in the Renaissance. This illustration is from Guglielmo Ebreo's *Treatise on the Art of Dancing* (1463). The central figure is probably Guglielmo, one of the most famous dancing masters of the fifteenth century.

courtly skills. Most dancing masters were Italian; one of the fifteenth century's most famous masters was Guglielmo Ebreo (William the Jew). In 1463, he wrote *A Treatise on the Art of Dancing*, which detailed the steps and movements for courtly dances and balls and described the qualities that skillful dancers should possess, including a sense of rhythm, a good memory, and a graceful manner.

The dances done by courtiers during the Renaissance were of two kinds. The *basse danse*, or low dance, included many poses and used gliding and hip-swaying steps. The feet never left the floor, as in the stately, ceremonial pavane, which may be named for the peacock (*paon* in French). *Haute danse*, or high dance, required quick leg movements and tiny running steps; the men did jumps, the women little hops. Men also did the more virtuosic movements — leaps, kicks, and the crossing of the feet in midair. Examples of *haute danse* were the lively triple-time galliard, the branles (our word *brawl* is derived from the name of this round dance, which involved violent shaking), and the volta. An early forerunner of the waltz, the volta was considered risqué in its time. In one of its movements, the gentleman lifted his partner by placing one hand under her bottom, then whirled her around, skirts flying in the air.

Dancing and spectacle had become so much a part of aristocratic life in the Renaissance that it would not be long before they joined together in *ballet de cour*, the ancestor of modern ballet.

# A Ballet Fit for a Queen

atherine de' Medici (1519–1589) learned the love of pageants, dancing, and spectacle from her father, Lorenzo II, duke of Urbino, a great patron of the arts. In 1533, the fourteen-year-old Catherine married the duke of Orléans, who in 1547 was crowned King Henry II of France.

Catherine was the mother of three kings of France: Francis II, Charles IX, and Henry III, and she exerted considerable control during the thirty years they reigned, a period of great religious and political conflict. As queen mother, Catherine, who is said to have introduced cosmetics, ice cream, lettuce, and artichokes into her adopted country, became known for her lavish entertainments, which she used to enhance her political power and impress visiting ambassadors. Her court became the center of European culture and set the standard for polite behavior and manners all over Europe.

*Ballet de cour*, or court ballet, was born at Catherine's glittering palace on a Sunday evening, October 15, 1581. The *Ballet Comique de la Reine (The Queen's Dramatic Ballet)* was presented in honor of the marriage of the queen's sister Margaret of Lorraine to the duke of Joyeuse.

*Ballet de cour* is considered the forerunner of modern ballet because for the first time, it logically combined mime, music, and dancing in one performance to tell one story. The production was conceived and directed by the queen's Italian violinist and dancing master, Balthasar de Beaujoyeulx. It told the story of Circe, the evil enchantress of ancient Greek legend, who is brought down by the powers of the gods and, in this version, by the majesty of the French king and queen. Although the musicians were professionals, all the dancers and players in the ballet were amateurs, chosen from among the members of the court.

This singular spectacular (it was performed only once) began shortly after ten P.M. in a vast hall of the Petit-Bourbon Palace, near the Louvre. Nine to ten thousand important guests were assembled in tiered galleries and balconies around three sides of the room; the royal family sat on a canopied platform along the fourth. The sumptuously costumed performers representing characters from classical

The hall and gallery, the *Ballet Comique de la Reine*, showing the tiers of spectators, the freestanding three-dimensional papier-mâché scenery for Pan's Grove and Circe's Palace, and the Golden Vault for the musicians.

mythology entered the hall on magnificently decorated floats and chariots. The performance lasted a marathon five hours, ending with a grand ballet, in which the audience and the performers, still in costume, danced together.

It is not known exactly what steps and patterns were performed in the *Ballet Comique de la Reine*, but we do know that they closely resembled the stately social dances of the day. Because the dances were performed in the center of the room and meant to be seen from above, the individual steps were not as important as the overall patterns. These were based on combinations of geometric designs and figure — squares, circles, ovals, triangles — that had symbolic meanings for the audience. For example, dancers forming two triangles within a circle represented a monarch's supreme power.

Although the *Ballet Comique de la Reine* cost several million francs, a sum that nearly bankrupted the French court, it was considered a great political and social success. It was widely imitated throughout Europe, although on a much less extravagant scale. An evening of dances, music, song, and verses performed in costume would be created around a theme such as the different kinds of love, the hours of the day, or mythological tales. *Ballet de cour* would rise to its greatest heights at the magnificent court of the ruler who also brought absolute monarchy to its height in Europe: Louis XIV, the Sun King.

## *The English Masque*

Across the English Channel, another form of court ballet, called the masque, developed, first becoming popular at the Tudor court of Henry VIII (1491–1547). Masques combined spectacular scenic devices with song, drama, and dance and were performed, usually only once, at royal banquets.

As in French *ballet de cour,* elaborately masked and costumed courtiers and musicians entered the room in a stately procession, then performed specially prepared dances. Next came revels, or spirited social dancing, in which the spectators were invited to participate. A final courtly dance by the masquers, done to music commissioned for the occasion, concluded the evening.

English masques became noted for the high quality of their librettos (the spoken or sung portions) and their scenic effects. The famous poet-dramatist Ben Jonson wrote over thirty masques, and one of England's first great architects, Inigo Jones, designed and supervised hundreds of masques over a period of thirty-five years. For one masque, he created a giant revolving globe; for another, a vision of hell, complete with smoke and flames, magically transformed into a vision of heaven circled with light.

In 1619, at the request of King James I, Inigo Jones began to build a special place for royal masques, the banqueting hall at Whitehall. It still exists today. But these elaborate entertainments came to an end only twenty-two years later, when England was plunged into a civil war that led to a temporary abolition of the monarchy. During the Commonwealth period, when Oliver Cromwell and the Puritans held sway, theatrical performances of any kind were frowned upon.

## Chapter 2

# A Dancing King Founds a Dancing School

Louis XIV (1638–1715) ruled over the richest, most magnificent, most powerful state in Europe for seventy-two years. His court at Versailles Palace, home to five thousand aristocrats and nobles, was one of the most elegant and theatrical in history. It was dominated by strict etiquette, majestic pomp, and pageantry. The king's day — from the moment his servants and courtiers woke him until he was undressed and put to bed by the same retinue — was a series of public theatrical events, with Louis as the main performer. The king took dance lessons every day and was accomplished in this art.

Court ballets often took as their theme the power and majesty of royalty, emphasizing the king's divine right to rule. Louis XIV had first participated in these elaborate spectacles as a child.

Tall, well built, with shapely legs and splendid chestnut-colored hair, the king was a dignified yet vigorous dancer. As he grew older, however, he also grew fatter, and he finally stopped performing altogether in court entertainments. When the king stopped participating in court ballets, so did the members of his court. But the monarch still loved to watch ballets, and it is during his reign and under his patronage that ballet began to change from a pastime for noble amateurs into an art for professionals. A way now had to be found to supply trained dancers who could perform to the high standards demanded by the king. Professional dancers did exist in France, but they were, for the most part, acrobats who performed at fairs or other common entertainments. Like the actors of the day, these dancers were not considered to be respectable.

In 1661, Louis XIV founded the Royal Academy of Dance, whose main concern was arranging and teaching social dances to members of the court. Eight years later, he founded the Royal Academy of Music, which was given the exclusive right to present operas and opera-ballets and which soon included its own school of dance to train the professionals needed for these productions. These two royal academies merged in 1672 and are known today as the Paris Opera — which has the oldest dancing school in existence.

Two men were important in the Royal Academy of Music and Dance. Choreographer Pierre Beauchamp (1636–1705), descended from a long line of artists, was born in the palace at Versailles. The inventor of the pirouette and the aerial turn, he was considered the greatest dancer of his day. He was Louis XIV's dancing master for more than twenty years, and in 1671, he was appointed superintendent of the king's ballets. It was Beauchamp who named and stan-

King Louis XIV of France costumed in cloth of gold for the role of Apollo, Le Roi Soleil (The Sun King). The young king was fourteen years old when he first danced this role in *The Ballet of the Night* (1652), a thirteen-hour *ballet de cour* that began at sunset and ended at dawn.

# The Five Positions of Classical Ballet

All ballet movements begin and end in one of the five positions:

There are also five basic positions of the arms, although these may vary slightly depending on the ballet method (French, Russian, Italian) being taught:

First Position

First position: With heels together, the legs and feet are turned out from the hips so that the feet form a straight line. Since the feet are turned out 90 degrees from parallel position, this is known as 90-degree turnout.

The arms, gently curved, are held low before the body.

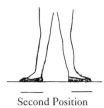

Second Position

Second position: Legs and feet are turned out from the hips, the feet forming a straight line, but with the heels separated by a distance equal to the length of one of the feet.

The arms are extended to the sides at shoulder height.

Third Position

Third position: With legs and feet turned out from the hips, one foot is placed directly in front of the other, with each heel touching the middle of the other foot.

One arm is curved overhead, the other extended to the side as in second position.

Fourth position: With legs and feet turned out from the hips, one foot is placed in front of the other, separated by a distance equal to the length of one of the feet, the heel of one foot in line with the toes of the other.

One arm is rounded in front of the chest, the other extended to the side.

Fourth Position

Fifth position: With the legs and feet turned out from the hips, one foot is placed directly in front of the other, with each heel touching the toes of the other foot.

Both arms are curved overhead.

Fifth Position

---

dardized the five basic positions of the feet that are the foundation for all ballet technique. By helping to formalize and codify ballet technique, he was one of the founders of the *ballet d'école*, or academic ballet. Because this codification occurred in France, most ballet terms are still called by their French names all over the world.

Composer Jean-Baptiste Lully (1632–1687) was the son of Italian peasants. Brought to France as a boy, he became a page in an aristocratic household at the age of fourteen. Through his talent as a violinist, he came to the attention of the king, and before he was twenty, he was named the king's royal composer of music. Lully's control over who would perform and what would be performed became as absolute as the king's control over the country. For many years, Lully and Beauchamp collaborated with France's great playwright Molière, creating court ballets, opera-ballets, and other entertainments.

Even though dancers were now professionals, not courtiers or royalty, ballets continued to be a reflection of polite behavior and society. Dancers at the Academy were taught how to present themselves and how to act and move like aristocrats. They were taught how to walk with legs and feet turned out to show off their fancily decorated heeled shoes. They learned how to bow, how to elegantly point their feet, and how to carry their bodies and use their arms and hands with grace, symmetry, and harmony. These stylized movements and poses of formal courtly demeanor are still part of classical ballet performed today.

Now that ballets were the province of professionals, other changes took place that began to alter how and where people viewed ballet. The king gave permission for ballets to be shown to the public in a magnificent theater that had once belonged to Cardinal Richelieu. This theater's performance area was a raised stage framed by a proscenium arch. Dancers now performed above rather than below the audience and could be seen only from the front. Ballet was ready to expand from stately floor patterns into an exploration of vertical space and aerial display. As a result, the dancers' turnout from the hip (the legs and feet facing toward the sides rather than the front) became even more important. Not only was this turnout considered to give their bodies a more pleasing line; it made it easier to move quickly and rhythmically in any direction and to perform the more elaborate and exciting steps that were being devised.

Although ladies had appeared in *ballet de cour,* it was thought improper for women to appear on a stage. At first, ballets performed in public could be danced only by men. It was easy for boys to play the female roles because all dancers were masked and wore wigs and often bulky costumes. In 1681, in the opera-ballet *Le Triomphe de l'Amour (The Triumph of Love)*, Lully introduced the first professional women dancers in French ballet. Four women had trained at the Academy, and the soloist, Mademoiselle Lafontaine, became the first recorded ballerina in history. Women were now to play a much larger role in the story of ballet.

# Part II

# The Eighteenth Century

Costume for a ballerina, c. 1750, modeled after the
court dress of the day: lavishly beribboned hooped
gowns that could be as wide as six feet.

## The Perfect Dance

The perfect dance needs music sweet
As dreams; seductive, so the feet
Are led to move as by some spell;
Or music as of murmuring shell.
True dance shows naught of haste or heat,
Nor trick, nor any kind of cheat.
Beauty and Joy, twin souls, should meet
To make that lovely miracle —
The perfect dance.

A field of wind-kissed waving wheat;
A swaying sea, scarce waked to greet
The dawn; clouds drifting; these things tell
What dance may be — if it excel.

Men said they saw in hers complete —
The perfect dance.

— Anonymous
1720, France

*Chapter 3*

# Some Modest Attempts at Change

In the decades following Louis XIV's retirement from dancing, ballet moved from the court to the public stage, becoming an entertainment enjoyed by merchants and shopkeepers as well as the nobility. At the same time, it was becoming less creative and its rules even more rigid, formal, and stylized. By 1687, the year of Lully's death, ballet as an art had gone into decline. By the early 1700s, ballets were no longer independent entertainments. More popular were the opera-ballets, in which dancing was secondary to the singing. Suites of dances, called divertissements, which were unrelated to the rest of the production, were used as interludes in the action of the opera. They could be inserted into any act and were often just an excuse to showcase popular dancers.

Ballet costumes had changed little from Lully's time. If anything, they had become even more exaggerated. Elaborately decorated court dress, featuring heavy floor-length hooped skirts, hindered rather than enhanced a ballerina's movements. The men, in their silk knee breeches and stockings, had a bit more freedom of movement, but their costumes included a stiff skirt called a *tonnelet*, which resembled the classical tutu worn by ballerinas today. All dancers were further hampered by padding and wigs, worn to make them look larger on stage. Dancers also had to wear the traditional theatrical masks, which hid any facial expression. Sometimes they had to dance while carrying the symbols of the characters they represented.

Costume for a danseur, c. 1750. Ornate costumes for men, along with wigs and plumed headdresses, were features of ballet in the mid–eighteenth century.

For example, a dancer portraying Diana, goddess of the moon and the hunt, carried a bow and a quiver of jeweled arrows and balanced a sparkling crescent moon on her head. If ballet was to regain its prominence as a serious art form, some changes were needed.

Marie Sallé (1707–1756) and Marie-Anne Cupis de Camargo (1710–1770) — the prima ballerinas of their day — were the first to defy tradition. Their small attempts at reform both scandalized and delighted their audiences. Contemporary writers called Sallé "a muse of gracious, modest gesture" and praised her dramatic spiritual expression, her eloquent, realistic acting and pantomime, and her unaffected, graceful style. Camargo was known for her dazzling allegro technique — fast steps, jumps, and turns. She was also the first ballerina to do steps previously done only by men, including the *entrechat quatre*, a jump during which the feet quickly cross four times, and the cabriole, a dramatic high-kicking jump. Each of these dancers had her own claque of admirers who thought that "their" ballerina was the best.

Marie Sallé was a child prodigy: she was not yet ten when she first danced professionally. Born into a large family of traveling Italian actors and acrobats, she was very young when she learned the expressive pantomime that, along with her refined and spiritual dancing, was to become her trademark.

When Sallé made her debut at the Paris Opera at the age of twenty, the backstage atmosphere of the ballet world was one of scandal and intrigue. Dancers were expected to flaunt both their jewelry and their lovers in public. But Sallé was a model of modesty and grace both in her private life and on stage. When not dancing, she spent most of her time with the celebrated writers, poets, and painters of the day.

Sallé was popular with audiences, but her opinions about costumes and the form that ballet should take were not popular among dancers or with the director of the Paris Opera. She believed ballet should be more than a display of skillful technique. She felt it should be graceful, expressive, and dramatic as well. Sallé was a proponent

Marie Sallé at the height of her fame, 1732. The etching, after a painting by Nicholas Lancret, shows Sallé as Diana, Goddess of the Moon, accompanied by the Three Graces and musicians.

of *ballet d'action*, or narrative ballet, in which all of a performance's aspects — music, steps, decor, and costumes — combine to tell the story, which follows a sensible, understandable plot. She wanted as much attention to be paid to truthful emotion as to bravura dancing. The costumes, realistically representing the period in which the ballet is set, should not stifle the dancers' movements. She was not allowed to put her theories into practice at the Royal Academy, so she crossed the English Channel to dance in London, a more liberal city whose theatergoers were open to new ideas.

On Valentine's Day, 1734, at London's Covent Garden theater, Sallé caused a sensation when she danced the role of Galatea in *Pygmalion*, a ballet she had choreographed and arranged. *Pygmalion* was based on the Greek myth about a sculptor who falls in love with his creation — a statue of a woman — and brings it to life.

Her costume startled the audience. Over a corset and a simple petticoat, she wore a figure-revealing, thin muslin tunic, which "draped about her in the manner of a Greek statue" as one eyewitness described it. Her unadorned hair fell freely over her shoulders. Despite the success of *Pygmalion*, it would take many more years for Sallé's modest innovations to be accepted by other dancers and ballet masters.

Marie-Anne Cupis de Camargo was a complete artistic and personal contrast to Marie Sallé. Born in Brussels, the daughter of a dancing master and violinist, she took her name from her grandmother, a Spanish noblewoman. Camargo made her debut at the Paris Opera at the age of sixteen. News of her astounding technical accomplishments had already preceded her, for she had been named prima ballerina at the Rouen Opera the year before. One story says she became an instant star when, as a member of the corps, she improvised a dance after the principal male dancer did not appear on cue for his variation. Like the movie stars and rock idols of today, she influenced fashion — everyone wanted to dress "à la Camargo." Hairstyles, hats, shoes, and gowns were all named after her. Camargo

Marie-Anne Cupis de Camargo, Sallé's rival at the Paris Opera, in a stylized peasant costume. Although her dress seems long and modest to us, it was considered shockingly short because it showed her leg above the ankle.

was such a popular dancer that her name became synonymous with eighteenth-century ballet and her life was the subject of both a ballet and an opera.

By modern standards, Camargo's technical ability might not be considered extraordinary, but spectators at that time were thrilled by her speed, agility, elevation, and airiness. Proud of her accomplishments, it was no wonder that around 1730 she decided to lower the heels of her dancing slippers so she could jump higher and to shorten her skirts a few inches so her rapidly moving feet could be seen and appreciated. The sight of even a few inches of a ballerina's leg and ankle was considered indecent. So Camargo wore a new piece of clothing under her skirts, the *caleçon de précaution,* a pair of close-fitting knickers, the predecessor of today's body-hugging tights.

The modest reforms suggested by Sallé and Camargo would not become accepted practice for many more years. It would take the work of several important ballet masters and the upheavals of the French Revolution to bring about the long-needed changes.

## Chapter 4

# The Father of Modern Ballet and His Followers

Jean-Georges Noverre (1727–1810), known as the Father of Modern Ballet, was a dancer, choreographer, ballet master, and teacher. For most of his life, this reformer was treated as an outsider by the conservative ballet establishment at the Royal Academy, and for many years he had to work outside of Paris, in cities all over Europe. In Vienna, as ballet master of the Imperial Theater, he taught dancing to Empress Maria Theresa and her daughter Marie Antoinette, who on becoming queen of France, finally got Noverre the coveted appointment to the Paris Opera.

Noverre was ballet's first great theorist. He thought that the art was losing itself in whirlings, pirouettes, and awkward spins. It had become too trivial and artificial, too concerned with displays of technical achievement just for the sake of virtuosity. Noverre had danced in Sallé's ballets, and he was influenced by her work. He championed the *ballet d'action*, believing that all parts of the ballet should work in harmony as a unified and coherent whole. Music, steps, costumes, scenery, pantomime — all should be directly related to the ballet's plot. Noverre collaborated with the great composers of his day, including Christoph Gluck and Wolfgang Amadeus Mozart — who were both trying to make the same kinds of reforms to opera — to create over 150 ballets. Unfortunately, none of his works have survived.

In 1760, Noverre published one of the most important books in ballet history, *Letters on the Dance and Ballet*, which contained his philosophy and advice. Noverre believed that expressiveness was as important as technical skill for a dancer. Every part of a dancer's body should be used to convey emotion and character. To nurture expressive movement and natural gesture, Noverre called for some revolutionary changes.

Noverre advised dancers to discard their enormous wigs, headdresses, and padding because they hid the face and distorted and concealed the natural line of the body. "A dancer's arms will speak in vain if his face be unmoved," wrote Noverre, and in 1772, the first dancer appeared unmasked on the Paris Opera stage. Noverre advocated "light and simple draperies of contrasting colors, worn in such a manner to reveal the figure," and allowing "free and unfettered movement."

Noverre's innovative reforms would eventually be adopted by ballet companies all across Europe through the work of his many pupils and followers, including Jean Dauberval (1742–1806) and Charles Didelot (1767–1837). In 1789, a few days before the storming of the Bastille, Dauberval presented the first comic ballet and the first with real-life characters, rather than the gods and goddesses of classical myth, as its central figures. His *La Fille Mal Gardée (The Poorly Guarded Girl)* is a comic love story, a picturesque look at contemporary French peasant life that combined folk dances and popular tunes with classical ballet steps and music. In many different versions, this ballet is still being danced today all over the world.

Charles Didelot, known as the Father of Russian Ballet, was a brilliant dancer as well as an innovative ballet master and teacher. His novel stage effects helped ballet literally take flight. After working in Paris and London, he was associated with the Imperial Ballet

School in St. Petersburg for nearly thirty years, having gone there in 1801 at the invitation of Czar Paul I.

On July 7, 1796, at the King's Theatre in London, audiences gasped in amazement as a ballerina first poised and balanced on demi-pointe (half-toes), then appeared to run a few steps on her toes before she rose above the footlights and flew in circles high across the stage! This small intimation of dancing *sur les pointes* (on the toes), which would become the hallmark of ballet in the next century, was Charles Didelot's idea. *Flore et Zéphyre (Flora and Zephyr),* his one-act ballet about the love between the Goddess of Flowers and the West Wind, used nearly invisible wires and counterweights to lift the ballerina in a realistic depiction of flight.

Although alarmed critics issued warnings and dancers demanded extra wages to perform flights in aerial ballets, Didelot continued to experiment with the new apparatus. He was soon sending whole flocks of dancers soaring, keeping them aloft for several minutes at a time.

## Three Dancing Styles

Dancers in the late eighteenth century did not all receive the same type of training. Based on their physiques, they were typecast as to the roles they could dance. Three different styles of dancing were taught: the noble, the *demi-caractère*, and the *caractère*. These styles can still be seen today, but ballet dancers now receive training that allows them to perform in any manner required by the choreography.

The noble style incorporates the slow adagio movements in a classical pas de deux: elegant, extended arabesques and ports de bras, supported pirouettes, and graceful lifts. It is fluid, harmonious dancing that is regal and dignified. Heroes and heroines of the ballet dance in the noble style.

The *demi-caractère*, or demi-character, style combines acting ability and technical skill. Still elegant and classical in nature, it is filled with lively allegro movements.

The *caractère*, or character, style is used in the folk or national dances (Spanish, Russian, Italian, Hungarian, Polish) that appear in many story ballets. Instead of toe shoes or ballet slippers, dancers wear soft boots or heeled shoes

Didelot is also known for his original choreography for the corps de ballet. He was one of the first to emphasize the different attributes that the ballerina and her partner, the danseur, bring to the pas de deux. His choreography for this male-female "conversation" employed lifts and jumps that emphasized male strength and rapid yet delicate steps that accentuated female grace and airiness. While Noverre and his followers were instituting their reforms, the political and social upheaval caused by the French Revolution (1789–1795) also led to drastic changes in ballet costumes.

After Louis XVI and Marie Antoinette were guillotined, any style of dress associated with royalty was not only unpopular but even dangerous — anything reminiscent of the excesses of the court was considered treasonable. Simplicity and equality of dress for both men and women was now the fashion, as plain clothing became identified with the new democratic ways of thinking. Instead of the knee breeches associated with the aristocracy, men began to favor trousers, a style previously worn only by sailors and farmers. Women wore the informal *robe en chemise*, a high-waisted, sometimes low-cut dress that looked more like a nightgown than outdoor wear. Made of thin white muslin or cotton calico, these gowns, with their long, straight folds, were designed to imitate ancient Greek dress, in a neoclassical, or new classical, style inspired by the archaeological discoveries being made at the time in Greece and Italy. The gowns, which fashionable women dampened to make them cling to the body, were often made of a material so transparent that white or pink silk tights had to be worn underneath.

Ballet costumes also became simpler and adopted a more natural, classical look. Costumes now allowed for greater freedom of movement, and this led to more innovations in ballet technique, especially for women. Male and female dancers might wear versions of the flowing Greek chiton, or tunic, over a maillot, the tights named after the Paris Opera costumer-tailor who invented them. Or the ballerina might don an Empire gown — a simple, flowing dress with a low neckline and high waist. Male dancers, having discarded the *tonnelet*, could also wear a costume inspired by Renaissance paintings — tights or thigh-high breeches, a short vest or jacket, billowing shirt, and soft boots. The influence of the ancient Greeks and Romans was also seen in the dancers' footwear. Decorated heeled leather shoes were replaced by softer and heelless sandal-like slippers, laced up the leg with a crisscross of ribbons.

# Part III

# The Nineteenth Century

Carlotta Grisi and her husband, danseur and ballet master Jules Perrot, in *Esmeralda* (1844), his ballet based on Victor Hugo's novel *The Hunchback of Notre Dame.*

'Twas an evening of beauty; the air was
   perfume,
The earth was all greenness, the trees were
   all bloom;
And softly the delicate viol was heard,
Like the murmur of love or the notes of a
   bird.

And beautiful maidens moved down in the
   dance,
With the magic of motion and sunshine of
   glance;
And white arms wreathed lightly, and
   tresses fell free
As the plumage of birds in some tropical
   tree.

              — John Greenleaf Whittier
           From "The Cities of the Plain"

*Chapter 5*

# The Revolution of Romanticism

During the closing years of the eighteenth century and early decades of the nineteenth, political, economic, artistic, and social revolutions were sweeping away the old structures of society. The American and French revolutions had fired people's imaginations with radical and visionary ideas of freedom and liberty. Napoleon's armies of conquest were redrawing the borders of Europe. Wars of national liberation were being fought from Greece to South America.

The Industrial Revolution was changing the way people earned their livings. Great machines were being invented to do the work that had been done by human or animal labor for centuries. The factory, not the home, was becoming the center of production. People were moving into the cities from their farms and villages in the countryside. Men, women, and even young children were forced to toil in the great urban factories and foundries to make a living. Although bankers, mill owners, merchants, and shopkeepers all benefited from the new economic changes, many others lived lives of misery and economic hardship.

The artistic world was also ready for its own revolution. The eighteenth century had been called the Age of Enlightenment and the Age of Reason, a period when the artistic and social standard of perfection was mathematical order, moderation, classicism, and an aristocratic approach to life. But these ideals did not seem appropriate for the new century that had been born in so much pain, passion, and turbulence. Nineteenth-century artists needed a new way to describe and explain their world. That new vision, which began in Germany but soon spread throughout Europe and to America, is called Romanticism. Literature, painting, and music were all affected by its sentiments. Ballet, a fusion of all these arts, was profoundly and forever changed by the Romantic philosophy.

Filled with brighter hopes for the future and inspired by the political revolutions going on around them, Romantic writers emphasized the rights of the individual and personal freedom. The artist was seen as a remote hero whose aim was self-expression. The artistic vision no longer reflected the cold, artificial, sophisticated world of the aristocrat but was warm, passionate, and full of feeling. Romantic artists, writers, and composers chose to explore highly emotional subjects: love, death, betrayal, heroism, revenge, untamed nature, the search for the ideal, and the redeeming power of sacrifice, as well as conflicts between good and evil, the flesh and the spirit, reality and the supernatural.

In an effort to go beyond the often unpleasant everyday reality of the world around them, the Romantics escaped in their imagination to faraway lands or into history, looking for exotic, alluring, and colorful backgrounds for their works. They longed for a simpler time, but one that contained the exotic adventure and the miracles that their own age lacked. Artists and writers rediscovered the Middle Ages — the beauty of the soaring Gothic cathedrals, the graceful behavior prescribed by the code of chivalry, the shivery excitement of a ruined abbey in the moonlight.

This interest in the melodramatic also led writers to an obsession with the folklore of their native lands. Old wives' tales and legends became the inspiration for plays, poems, and ballets. The literary world was soon filled with supernatural spirits of the air,

water, and woods — sprites, elves, ghosts, the enchanted princesses and spell-casting wizards of fairy tales.

Almost overnight, the Romantic philosophy changed and revitalized every aspect of ballet — its stories, scenery, costume, music, choreography, technique, and most of all, the role of the ballerina. She was now to take center stage as the supreme personification of the art. A delicate, pale, unearthly being, she would become the Romantics' idealized vision of all womankind.

## Setting the Stage

Innovations and changes in stagecraft during the first half of the nineteenth century helped bring about the theatrical magic of Romantic ballets.

Until gaslights were introduced in London in 1817, theaters and opera houses had been lit by smoky candles, kerosene lamps, or natural light, sources that could not be controlled. Gaslight could be dimmed or brightened as needed. It realistically simulated the illusions of moonlight or dawn so necessary for the Romantic *ballets blancs*, those "white ballets" that transported audiences far away from the gritty reality of city life. And for the first time in a theater, the house lights in the auditorium could be lowered before the performance began, adding to the sense of expectation and magic. The house lights stayed dim throughout the ballet, creating a feeling of separation between the audience sitting in the semidarkness and what was happening on the brightly lit stage. The theatrical magic was further enhanced in 1829, when it became the custom to close the curtains between scenes.

There was one drawback to gaslight: the tragedy of an increasing number of theater fires. In 1862, Emma Livry, a young protégée of

Marie Taglioni, died a horrible death because of a gaslight fire. Waiting in the wings during a rehearsal, she stood too close to an open gas jet, and her costume caught fire. She suffered for almost a year before dying from her burns.

At about the same time that gaslight was being introduced, theaters also started to use curved mirrors and calcium oxide (a chemical compound that produces a radiant white light when heated to high temperatures) to make limelight, a spotlight of intense brilliance. Later, in 1846, arc lights, powered by electric currents and carbon rods, were used for the first time at the Paris Opera for similar effects. Theaters did not become fully electrified until the early 1880s. The first American theater to use incandescent lighting, inside and out, was the Bijou in Boston, in 1882.

## Chapter 6

# The Birth of Romantic Ballet

On November 22, 1831, when the Paris Opera curtain rose on the "Ballet of the Nuns," which opened the third act of Giacomo Meyerbeer's opera *Robert le Diable (Robert the Devil)*, no one in the audience had any idea that ballet was about to be changed forever. Revealed in the flickering gaslight was a ruined abbey bathed in the soft glow of moonlight, with the ghostly spirits of nuns, robed and veiled in white, rising up from their graves, dancing with abandon. In both subject matter and scenic effects, this was unlike any ballet ever seen before. Marie Taglioni (1804–1884), the young ballerina who danced the Abbess, moved so lightly and with such grace that she seemed to be floating above the stage.

Several months later, on March 12, 1832, Taglioni danced the title role in the first full-length Romantic ballet, *La Sylphide*, choreographed by her father, Filippo (1777–1871). *La Sylphide* began a new era of choreography that is still remembered as the Golden Age. It embodied many of the elements of the Romantic era.

Set in Scotland's misty Highlands and based on a Scottish folktale, *La Sylphide* tells the tragic story of an elusive creature of the air and woods, the winged Sylph, who enchants James, a prosperous young farmer soon to be married. James, spellbound, abandons his bride on their wedding day in an attempt to capture and possess this otherworldly vision. But mortal man cannot possess an unattainable ideal. In Act II, when James finally traps the Sylph, it means her

Marie Taglioni as the Sylph and her brother Paul as James, in *La Sylphide* (1832), the first full-length ballet of the Romantic era.

death. If she cannot escape the bounds of earth, she can no longer exist.

The ballet ideally fitted the talents of Marie Taglioni, whose pale, elfin features and demure, childlike smile were enhanced by the gaslight. Her dancing was lyrical and spiritual. She had the ability to skim, apparently weightlessly, across the stage. Her high jumps ended in gossamer-soft landings. She personified a sense of shimmering magic and poetic mystery.

Taglioni's costume, designed especially for her by the painter Eugène Lami, established the "uniform" of the Romantic ballerina. Encircling her head was a small wreath of flowers; her hair was simply parted down the middle and tied in back. The unadorned, tight bodice of her dress showed off her pale neck and shoulders and her softly rounded arms; the mid-calf-length bell-shape skirt of diaphanous white gauze revealed her ankles and feet. Taglioni's Romantic tutu, which gave her complete liberty of movement and enhanced the beauty of her arabesques and leaps, gave the *ballets blancs*, or "white ballets," their name.

*La Sylphide* was an overnight success. Taglioni, already the darling of Parisian society, became the rage of Europe. Because of her, ballets and ballet dancers would now have a different look. All ballerinas had to be sylphlike — pure, modest, idealized women who could rise above earthbound man. All ballets had to be filled with mystery, telling timeless stories of the conflict between good and evil, reality and fantasy. Heroines were not made of flesh and blood but were spiritual or supernatural visions far removed from everyday life; heroes aspired to an ideal love only to destroy it.

Male dancers now began a long descent from their previous importance. Soon their roles would become that of porter, restricted to supporting, carrying, or lifting the ballerina. By the second half of the century, many male roles were being danced by women in travesty, dressed in men's clothing.

## Marie Taglioni: A Sylph for All Seasons

When Marie Taglioni was a little girl, no one could have guessed that she would become one of the greatest ballerinas of all time. She was a prim little child, skinny and pale, with plain, sharp features. She was stoop-shouldered and had a very long neck and arms. Her early teachers didn't think she had any talent, and her classmates taunted her as "that little hunchback." One ballet master suggested to her mother that she learn to be a dressmaker because she would never be a good dancer. But Marie was destined for the stage: her Swedish grandmother was a well-known singer, her Italian grandfather, aunts, and uncles were distinguished dancers (as was her younger brother Paul), and her father, Filippo Taglioni, was one of the era's foremost dancers, teachers, and choreographers.

Filippo, known for his single-mindedness and iron discipline, took over his daughter's training when she was seventeen. Because Marie's body did not match the ideal for the voluptuous ballerinas of the day, her father began a grueling program of exercises and preparations to overcome her so-called physical "handicaps." Marie practiced six hours a day, every day, to the music of a violin. (Until the twentieth century, the violin, not the piano, was the instrument used to count out the beats and measures during ballet practice.) Her lessons often ended in tears of exhaustion. Sometimes Marie nearly fainted with fatigue, but the exer-

Marie Taglioni as the Sylph. Her pose — elbows bent, wrists crossed, head tilted to one side — was originally devised by her father, Filippo Taglioni, to camouflage her long neck and arms. He would also sometimes have her stand with her arms folded across her chest. Ever since, these poses have been associated with the Romantic ballerina and Romantic ballets.

cises gave her very strong legs and feet, enabling her to extend the techniques of pointe dancing. To improve her adagio technique, she would hold a pose on demi-pointe to the count of one hundred. She would practice unsupported pirouettes over and over. Her technique was so strong that during her soaring elevations, she seemed to hover in the air, defying the laws of gravity. It was said that it took her just three leaps to bound across the stage of the Paris Opera.

Marie Taglioni was not the first ballerina to dance on pointe, but she was the first to make it truly magical. She did not perform in the blocked toe shoes of today but in fragile, narrow tubelike slippers made of silk ribbon with paper-thin soles. She moved toe dancing beyond a display of garish acrobatics and tricks with wires and pulleys into a lofty realm that led the *London Times* to declare that ballet was now "an art to rank with poetry and painting."

During her long career, Marie Taglioni danced in hundreds of ballets, appearing in all the great capitals of Europe. She was the most famous performer of her day. After a triumphal appearance in Russia — the czar came every night — her adoring fans cooked her ballet slippers and served them in a sauce. She was the first ballerina to be showered with flowers at a curtain call. Following one performance in Paris, the curtain was unable to come down because of the thick carpet of roses, camellias, and violets thrown by admiring fans.

Marie Taglioni retired in 1848, at the age of forty-four. In 1860, she returned to the Paris Opera to choreograph her only ballet, *Le Papillon (The Butterfly)*, to Jacques Offenbach's first ballet score. Although she had made a fortune during her career, her last years were spent in poverty, teaching dancing and deportment to young ladies in London. The ballerina who had been worshipped and adored while she danced died penniless in Marseilles in 1884.

*Chapter 7* —

# Fairy Sprites and Fiery Beauties

During the 1830s and 1840s, Marie Taglioni was the acknowledged, crowned Queen of Dance, but it wasn't long before a rival for the title appeared. The rivalry was encouraged by the Paris newspapers and by the manager of the Paris Opera. He saw it as the perfect way to increase his box office receipts and generate excitement in the increasingly middle-class audience of soldiers, bureaucrats, shopkeepers, and their wives and daughters.

Fanny Elssler (1810–1884), an Austrian dancer, was six years younger than Taglioni. She had started dancing at the age of seven, and was in the corps de ballet when Taglioni made her debut in Vienna in 1822. Like Sallé and Camargo, who had competed for audience attention a hundred years earlier, Taglioni and Elssler were dancers of totally different styles.

While Taglioni was the embodiment of a spiritual, feminine ideal, Elssler, darkly beautiful and exotic, was a fiery dancer-actress of earthiness and sensuality. She excelled in dramatic demi-character roles and folk or national dances. Her most famous dance, first performed at the Paris Opera in 1836, was the seductive "La Cachucha." This Spanish-style dance was punctuated by clicking castanets and filled with heel tapping, quick footwork, intricate, precise pointe work, and bewitching twists and bends. Elssler attacked the stage with her toes, using her feet as percussion instruments. Taglioni, by contrast, never made a sound when she danced.

During the Romantic age, balletomanes, or ballet enthusiasts, clamored for more exciting and colorful ethnic national dances. Elssler obliged with Neapolitan tarantellas, Polish *cracoviennes*, and Gypsy *gitanas*.

Théophile Gautier, a journalist, poet, and the first major ballet critic, called Elssler's style "pagan" and said that she "dances with her whole body, from the top of her hair to the tips of her toes." Compared to her, he wrote, "the others are but a pair of legs struggling beneath a motionless body."

Fanny Elssler, Marie Taglioni's chief rival at the Paris Opera. Her fiery style, especially in the Spanish-flavored "La Cachucha" (pictured here) was the opposite of Taglioni's fragile, ethereal dancing.

Elssler was the first great Romantic ballerina to visit America, crossing the Atlantic in 1840 on the first passenger steamship. It was an eventful voyage: Elssler surprised a thief in her cabin about to steal her jewels. Alone and unarmed, she reacted with a strong ballet kick, which killed the intruder. Elssler toured America for two years, conquering audiences wherever she went. She was feted by society ladies in New York, Boston, and New Orleans. In Baltimore, adoring young men pulled her carriage through the streets to the theater each night. In Washington, Congress adjourned for her performances. With President Van Buren's son as her escort, Elssler was honored at a banquet, during which wine was drunk from her slipper. Shawls, corsets, and a soap were named for her; cigars and whiskey bottles bore her likeness.

The next dancer to capture the public's attention was a fair-haired, violet-eyed beauty from Italy. Carlotta Grisi (1819–1899) was a fearless dancer. One of her most famous roles called for her to throw herself off a platform over six feet high into the arms of her partner. Her talents combined Taglioni's unearthly fragility with Elssler's dramatic flair.

Carlotta Grisi was five when she first appeared on the stage of La Scala in Milan, dancing in a children's chorus. She was sixteen when Marie Taglioni's former partner, Jules Perrot, saw her dance in Naples. He soon became Grisi's teacher and partner, then, for seven years, her husband, the first of many men to fall in love with her. After they danced together in England, he brought her to France, where she made her debut at the Paris Opera in 1840 in an opera-ballet in which she also sang. One year later, on June 28, 1841, Grisi became the first Giselle, a role that to this day is considered one of the supreme tests of a dancer's dramatic ability and technical skill.

## *Jules Perrot: "The Male Taglioni"*

Jules Perrot (1810–1892) was the finest and most esteemed male dancer in an era when the ballerina ruled supreme. Perrot began his career as a circus pantomimist and comic dancer. While still a teenager, he began to study with Auguste Vestris (1760–1842), a celebrated classical dancer of the previous generation, who also taught Fanny Elssler and Charles Didelot. Vestris advised his homely young student to "jump about, turn, move around, but never give the public time to look at you closely," and Perrot became noted for his leaps, aerial turns, speed, and strength. Gautier called him "Perrot the airy, Perrot the sylph, Perrot the male Taglioni!" "Perrot is visible music," he wrote, "the greatest dancer in the world."

Perrot would also become one of the Romantic period's greatest choreographers, known for the way in which he presented dramatic themes through expressive dance and mime. *Esmeralda* (1844), his most successful ballet, was based on Victor Hugo's 1831 novel, *The Hunchback of Notre Dame*, although Perrot gave the tragic story a happy ending. Perrot was noted for the attention he paid to the individual talents of all his dancers. *Esmeralda*, which starred his wife, Carlotta Grisi, was the first ballet in which the realistically mimed crowd scenes were choreographed to give each member of the corps something different to do.

## Chapter 8

# A Ballet Called Giselle

*Giselle* was created quickly. It was the work of four men, each of them in love with Carlotta Grisi. The idea for the ballet came from Théophile Gautier, who would eventually marry Grisi's sister. The libretto, or story, was written by Count Vernoy de Saint-Georges; the music was composed by Adolphe Adam; Grisi's dances were choreographed by her husband, Jules Perrot, although he was not officially credited in the program. All of the choreography was attributed to Jean Coralli, the ballet master at the Paris Opera.

Gautier had come across an old German/Slavic legend that told of the *wili*s, ghosts of young girls who had died before their wedding day. The *wili*s were restless spirits that rose from their graves at midnight to dance in the woods, luring to their deaths young men who had betrayed their lovers.

Count Saint-Georges, a veteran librettist who had worked on many ballets and operas, quickly fashioned the legend into a two-act ballet whose themes of tragic love, betrayal, death, and forgiveness would satisfy the Romantic imagination.

Act I, set in a German village, features both joyous folk dances and the famous mad scene, in which Giselle, a young peasant girl, loses her reason and dies after being deceived by Prince Albrecht, who had promised to marry her. In Act II, set in a gloomy, supernatural forest, Giselle has become a *wili*, but her love for Albrecht saves him from the wraith of cruel Queen Myrtha and her sister spirits,

Carlotta Grisi, the first
Giselle (1841),
combined Taglioni's
unearthly delicacy
with Elssler's
dramatic flair.

who would dance the repentant lover to death for his betrayal. The
ballerina who dances Giselle must be an excellent actress. She has to
realistically convey, through dance and mime, emotions that range
from love to madness, from shyness to admiration, from happiness to
dismay. She must then become a creature from another world.

Adolphe Adam, who composed the score for *Giselle*, was another
theatrical veteran. His music for this work was different from any
other ballet music of the time. To help audiences understand the plot
and to heighten the drama, Adam devised several musical phrases or
melodies, called leitmotivs, to symbolize the character of Giselle.

Each time she appeared or danced, one of her leitmotivs was heard, but in a slightly different form. The musical changes represented the changes in her emotions or behavior. Jules Perrot carried the idea of leitmotivs over to his choreography by having Giselle repeat, in slightly different ways, the same series of steps and gestures.

During the Romantic period, ballet was an enormously popular form of entertainment. Reviews soon spread the word about *Giselle* beyond Paris; theatergoers in other cities wanted to see its beauty for themselves. Better roads and expanded and improved rail systems were making it easier than ever to travel, so it was not long before the ballet was performed in theaters throughout Europe, in Russia, and in the United States. *Giselle* has remained continually in the repertoires of the great ballet companies throughout the world for more than 150 years.

## Chapter 9

# A Choreographer from the North

he small country of Denmark has had a thriving ballet tradition for hundreds of years. In the 1600s, Danish kings delighted in French-style *ballet de cour*, and in 1748, Copenhagen's Royal Theatre was established. In 1816, Frenchman Antoine Bournonville, a pupil of Noverre, was appointed ballet master of the Royal Danish Ballet. He was succeeded by his son, Auguste Bournonville (1805–1879), a dancer, choreographer, and teacher. Auguste Bournonville developed an especially buoyant, fleet-footed style and technique that is still performed in his homeland.

Bournonville was an accomplished dancer and mime. A soloist at the Paris Opera, he appeared on stage until he was forty-three. In 1829, he returned to Copenhagen and began choreographing his own ballets and developing his distinctive style of dancing, which reflected the elegant traditions of eighteenth-century academic French ballet, taught to him by Auguste Vestris. In Paris, Bournonville had also been exposed to the darker and more passionate elements of Romanticism, but he had a sunny and optimistic view of life. His ballets are filled with wit and humor and have a freshness, joy, and charm that reflect the warm Danish outlook. Many of his ballets are comedies, or have happy endings.

The Bournonville style, which combines acting and dance, is neat and clear and is meant to look effortless, despite its difficulty. It stresses balance and harmony and emphasizes natural gestures that

The finale of Auguste Bournonville's *Napoli* depicts all the villagers, from the smallest children on up, in a joyous celebration reuniting the ballet's hero and heroine. The ballet has been performed by the Royal Danish Ballet since 1842.

intermingle with the dancing. The choreography is often filled with rapid changes of direction; big but quietly landed jumps (but not many pirouettes); high springy elevations (a quality called *ballon*); small, quick beats; and precise, clean, fast footwork. Bournonville dancers hold their upper bodies still, their arms curved but close to their sides or out wide, as if embracing the whole audience. Dances often end with sailing leaps toward the footlights.

Unlike other choreographers of the Romantic period, Bournonville did not neglect male dancers. He provided them with many strong aerial variations that contrasted with the dainty, graceful movements he gave his ballerinas. In fact Denmark was the only country where male dancers retained their importance during the supremacy of the Romantic ballerina.

During his long career, Bournonville created over fifty ballets. A dozen of them are still danced today. In 1836, he presented his own version of *La Sylphide*. Because he didn't have enough money to buy the music from the Paris Opera, he hired a twenty-year-old Danish nobleman, Herman Løvenskjold, to write a new score; it is this music that is used in all modern productions of the ballet. Bournonville's Sylph was his protégée, Lucile Grahn (1819–1907), a young dancer called "the Danish Taglioni." Blond, tall, slim, and beautiful, she combined strong technique and an aptitude for mime with a dreamy, effortless style.

Bournonville's ballets showed aspects of the Romantic spirit by displaying local color recorded from his travels around Europe. Bournonville created ballets set in Belgium, Greece, Norway, Russia, Spain, Italy, South America, and the Orient, as well as his native Denmark. One of his most famous is *Napoli* (1842), a picture of Italian peasant life on the shore of the Bay of Naples. It was the first ballet of the Romantic era to use authentic folk dances. He also made ballets from legends and fairy stories and from material about ordinary people in real situations. For example, *A Folk Tale* (1854), based on Norse myths, concerns trolls, elves, and babies switched at birth, and *The King's Volunteer Guards on Amager* (1871) recreates an entire early nineteenth-century town and its inhabitants.

Perhaps because Copenhagen was off the beaten path and Denmark was a relatively isolated country, the Bournonville tradition was preserved by his successors at the Royal Danish Ballet. Bournonville's *La Sylphide* is as authentic a depiction as we have of Romantic choreography of the Golden Age.

## Chapter 10

# A Teacher from the South

From the days of court ballets through the Romantic era, France was the artistic center of ballet. As early as the seventeenth century, however, Italy was also producing great ballet dancers and teachers. In the nineteenth century, Italy was the home of a dancer, choreographer, and teacher whose work became the standard for ballet instruction and training throughout all the dance capitals of Europe.

Born in Naples, Carlo Blasis (1797–1878) was principal dancer at Milan's La Scala Theater. At the age of twenty-three, he first set down his thoughts about ballet. Several years later, he wrote *The Code of Terpsichore*, the first comprehensive book on dancing technique. It became the textbook for every European dancing school and theater, influencing the development of what we now call classical ballet and forming the basis for many of today's teaching methods.

Blasis, who had studied with Jean Dauberval, was the son of a noble family and had been well educated in all the arts that constituted ballet — music, choreography, literature, drama, painting, sculpture, and even anatomy. In *The Code of Terpsichore*, Blasis looked scientifically at previous codes and rules of ballet (including Noverre's *Letters*) and then refined and improved on them, creating his own clear and simple drawings to complement his text. Like Noverre, he understood that it took more than just mastering the steps to make a great dancer.

Illustrations by Carlo Blasis from *The Code of Terpsichore* (1828), showing attitude, the position first described by the Italian ballet master in 1820. The attitude pose is often used in turning and promenades. Blasis used paintings and sculpture as his models for the perfect and harmonious dancer. Figure 1 on plate IX is of the Winged Mercury, the sixteenth-century sculpture by Giovanni da Bologna, which was Blasis's inspiration. Figure 4 shows a ballerina preparing for a pirouette. The dancers are wearing costumes influenced by classical Greece and Rome.

Believing in daily exercise and practice, he established a systematic training regimen still followed by students today. He specified the age when training should begin — between eight and twelve. He established the order for ballet classes — they should begin with barre exercises to develop balance, equilibrium, and strength, then go on to floor work to develop speed. He provided rules for doing proper pirouettes and pliés, arabesques and batteries. He insisted on a 90-degree turnout and on the importance of exercising all parts of the body equally. Blasis believed that learning mime was an important part of a dancer's education, because it was a means of building a total character on stage.

In 1837, Blasis and his wife, Annunziata, became codirectors of La Scala's Imperial Ballet Academy. Among the great Romantic ballerinas who studied with him were Carlotta Grisi, Lucile Grahn, and Fanny Cerrito (1817–1909). Cerrito, who was also a choreographer of six ballets, was nicknamed Ma'amselle Cherrytoes. She was tiny and plump, flamboyant and flirtatious, a Neapolitan ballerina whose speed and dashing pointe work came to epitomize the Italian style of ballet.

## "The Greatest Terpsichorean Exhibition That Was Ever Known"

Hundreds of ballets were staged between 1832 and 1850, the Golden Age of Romantic ballet. Most are completely forgotten; less than a handful are still danced today. But one, a divertissement of pure dance that was performed only four times in July of 1845 at Her Majesty's Theatre, London, made ballet history. It was such an unusual event that Queen Victoria, who loved ballet, and her husband, Prince Albert, were in the gala audience at the command performance on the third night.

The *Pas de Quatre* brought together four of the five greatest ballerinas of the Golden Age — Marie Taglioni, Lucile Grahn, Carlotta Grisi, and Fanny Cerrito. Only Fanny Elssler was missing, because her rivalry with Marie Taglioni was so bitter that the two would not appear on stage together. The idea for the ballet sprung from the mind of Benjamin Lumley, manager of Her Majesty's Theatre.

The *Pas de Quatre* (1845), one of the most famous divertissements in the history of ballet, brought together four great ballerinas of the Romantic age — Carlotta Grisi, Marie Taglioni, Lucile Grahn, and Fanny Cerrito.

Lumley asked Jules Perrot, ballet master at the theater since 1843, to devise the choreography for the *Pas de Quatre*. Perrot faced the difficult job of presenting four temperamental and very different prima ballerinas on the same stage and making all of them look their best.

Before the event, the *London Times* observed that it threatened to be "a collision that the most carelessly managed railroad could hardly hope to equal." Afterward they hailed it as "the greatest Terpsichorean exhibition that was ever known in Europe." How did Perrot and Lumley pull this off? There was no question that Taglioni would have the honor of dancing last, for she was, after all, the "first among equals" and the star of this all-star extravaganza. But who would dance right before her, the next most coveted position? Up until the day of the performance, arguments among the dancers drove Perrot to distraction and threatened to halt the proceedings altogether. Lumley, with the tact of a diplomat, solved the problem by deciding that the variations would be danced in order of age, with the youngest dancer going first. All agreed, but not before more disagreements about birth dates. Finally the show could go on to become ballet legend.

*Chapter 11*

# The Closing Years of the Romantic Era

No Golden Age lasts forever. From 1848 to 1849, a series of worker revolts caused by crop failures, famine, and unemployment swept across Europe. The next twenty years saw a period of strong nationalism and civil war. People still went to the ballet, but tastes were changing. By the 1860s, the great Romantic ballerinas — Taglioni, Grisi, Elssler, Grahn, and Cerrito — had retired. Serious composers were no longer interested in writing music for the ballet. Audiences, bored with the endless supernatural stories of ghostly visions and airborne sprites, wanted something new.

Writers, tired of looking to the Middle Ages, fairy tales, and legends for their inspiration, saw the present and the future as having more promise than the past. Charles Dickens, Harriet Beecher Stowe, and Emile Zola were writing realistic novels about real people with real problems. Artists such as Eduoard Manet, Pierre-Auguste Renoir, Claude Monet, and Edgar Degas were painting the world they saw around them. It was the age of the great international expositions of science, industry, and technological innovations. Mechanical and medical ingenuity enabled people to live longer and better lives. The world was shrinking as steam engines made high-speed train and ship travel possible. Theatrical performances reflected this sense of progress, energy, and confidence. Ballets came to feature stories about real people doing real things.

The ballet master at the Paris Opera was a shrewd businessman and a talented choreographer who knew how to satisfy the public's demand for novelty. Arthur Saint-Léon (1821–1870) was a Paris-born jack-of-all-trades. He had been a child prodigy on the violin and a graceful dancer who had partnered Taglioni and Grahn, as well as Fanny Cerrito, who was his wife from 1845 to 1851. He invented a system of dance notation (a way of recording a ballet in a written code), composed ballet music, and was sometimes called upon to make the costumes and scenery for his works. As a choreographer, Saint-Léon knew how to create ballets that reflected popular topics of conversation or events that were in the news. He was a master of light comedy and of choreographing lively national character dances.

Saint-Léon had succeeded Jules Perrot as ballet master at the Imperial Maryinsky Theatre in St. Petersburg, Russia, but he often returned to the Paris Opera during the summer months to stage his productions there. *Coppélia*, one of the great comic ballets of the nineteenth century, was his last ballet and his masterpiece; it premiered at the Paris Opera on May 25, 1870. Featuring a hero who yearns after an ideal love, the ballet contrasts elements of realistic local color with hints of magic and the supernatural. Although *Coppélia* was novel in many ways, it was the last gasp of the Romantic era, which had begun with *La Sylphide* in 1832. It would also mark the finale of France's ballet supremacy. Saint-Léon's libretto would, however, become the basis for the many versions of the ballet seen today.

*Coppélia, or The Girl with the Enamel Eyes*, is a ballet with a clever heroine, a silly hero, mechanical dolls, and a tragic-comic inventor. It is based on a story about a mad doll maker who wanted to create a doll with a soul. The author was E. T. A. Hoffmann (1776–1822), a German writer and composer known for his gothic tales of madness, horror, and the supernatural.

Saint-Léon took the macabre tale of Dr. Coppélius, set it in a

The doll Coppélia and her creator, Dr. Coppélius, in a scene from George Balanchine's production of *Coppélia* for the New York City Ballet. *Coppélia*, originally choreographed by Arthur Saint-Léon in 1870 for the Paris Opera, can be seen today in many different versions.

storybook village in Galicia, in what is now Poland, and turned it into a witty and sparkling romp with a happy ending. Franz, a young village boy, falls in love with Dr. Coppélius's creation, thinking she is a real girl. To cure him of this infatuation, his true beloved, Swanilda, sneaks into Dr. Coppélius's workshop, changes places with the doll, and proceeds to make fools of both Franz and the toy maker, who is also in love with his own creation. The ballet ends in a wedding divertissement, the lovers reunited.

*Coppélia* contains joyous Polish mazurkas and Hungarian czardas, as well as Scottish and Spanish numbers for Swanilda to dance when she pretends to be Coppélia. The sparkling music for *Coppélia* is by Léo Delibes, who used traditional ethnic tunes and melodic musical descriptions for the various characters, giving his score a colorful atmosphere and realistic feel.

For his Swanilda, Saint-Léon chose a sixteen-year-old Italian dancer, Giuseppina Bozzacchi (1853–1870). She had never appeared in public, but she was a strong, musical dancer whose warm, lively temperament was suited to the role. The part of Franz, which was mostly mime, was played by a woman in travesty (dressed as a man), a tradition the Paris Opera would follow for this ballet until the 1950s. *Coppélia* was a great success, and Bozzacchi was hailed as the new Carlotta Grisi. But a career in the limelight was not to be her fate. A few weeks after the premiere, the Franco-Prussian War broke out, and all the theaters, including the Opera, were closed. Paris was placed under siege, its inhabitants forced to live in horrifying conditions. Within three months, Saint-Léon, only forty-nine, was dead. Not long after, his Swanilda succumbed to smallpox and died on her seventeenth birthday.

The last years of the nineteenth century saw a decline in the quality of ballet throughout Western Europe. The Paris Opera had reopened in 1871, but the ballets, filled with uninspired choreography, were once again reduced to divertissements inserted into operas. Ballet at the Opera House during this period meant a pretty face in a skimpy costume. Performances were purely social, not artistic, events. In England, ballets were relegated to the music halls and the vaudeville stage. In Italy, La Scala's school was continuing to turn out technically brilliant dancers, but the ballets themselves took on spectacular circuslike dimensions.

Choreographer Luigi Manzotti (1835–1905) specialized in theatrical extravaganzas, whose like would not be seen again until the elaborate productions that have opened recent Olympic Games. Manzotti, who wrote his own scenarios and liked to put his dancers in daring costumes, wove his productions around grandiose themes.

*Excelsior,* performed over one hundred times at La Scala in 1881 and later produced in Paris, London, and St. Petersburg, was billed as an historical allegory in six parts and eleven scenes. The story it told was "The Progress of Mankind." A colorful, crowded display of fantastic stage effects and elaborate scenery, it had a cast of five hundred, including characters called Light and Civilization. In mime, processions, and synchronized dancing, it celebrated such technological advances as the telegraph, the opening of the Suez Canal, the invention of the steamboat, the discovery of electricity, the building of a tunnel through the Alps, and other examples of human ingenuity. Manzotti's other productions included a history of the world and the triumph of love (*Amor*, 1886), featuring 200 dancers, 250 non-dancing extras, 3000 costumes, 18 horses, 2 elephants, and an ox, and *Sport* (1897), a depiction of athletic pastimes from skating to big-game hunting.

There was one country, however, where ballet dancing was still considered a respected profession and ballet a creative and serious art. That country was the imperial Russia of the czars.

## Ballet Slippers

Pointe shoes are the universal symbol of the ballerina, the source of much of the magic that is ballet. Not only do they give the ballerina's leg an elongated, graceful line; they also enable her to dance with gravity-defying lightness and daring speed. Her special shoes are different from those worn by any other kind of dancer.

Ballet shoes have changed enormously since Marie Taglioni darned the tips of her flimsy silk slippers and padded them with cotton wool so she could balance on her toes for a few seconds. The blocked toe came into existence about 1860, and the stiffened pointe shoes of today became popular at the turn of the century.

Traditionally, pointe shoes are made almost entirely by hand, and today they are made almost exactly the way they were a hundred years

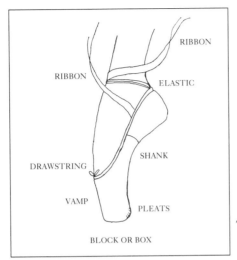

The Toe Shoe

ago. There is no right or left foot. The cobbler first cuts and sews the canvas- or cotton-backed satin uppers that form the pliable shank supporting the instep. The slippers, turned inside out, are then shaped around a last, a plastic or wooden mold of the foot. The next step is the most important — making the block, the square box that surrounds and supports the dancer's toes and helps her to balance on pointe. The block is made of papier-mâché-like layers of fabric, paper, and strong glue or paste. Each shoe company uses its own special adhesives; they also have their own way of constructing the block, and they guard these procedures like state secrets.

To make the shoe flexible, the material behind the toe is pleated and stitched down, then sewn to the thin leather outer sole. The shoe is now turned right side out. These turned shoes are sent on to another cobbler, who shapes the inside and outside of the shoe with his hands and pounds it with a smooth-edged hammer. Then he glues in an inner lining, sews in the drawstring, cuts crisscross lines on the sole for traction, and stamps on the maker's symbol. The shoes are then set on racks to dry for several days or are dried in large ovens overnight. Shoes that have not been allowed enough time to dry can collapse when worn.

Professional ballerinas may spend years trying to find the perfect shoe and the perfect shoemaker. Because pointe shoes have to fit like a second skin, ballerinas have their shoes made to order.

After she receives her toe shoes from the manufacturer, a ballerina still has work to do before she can use her slippers. Dancers are superstitious about the tedious task of sewing on the ankle ribbons and elastics that keep the shoes on securely and will not let anyone do it for them. Some prepare all the shoes they will need for a week; others work on their slippers only before each performance. They snip away material from the very tip of the toes. This area, on which the ballerina balances, is about the size of a half-dollar. Dancers reinforce the pointes by darning to provide a better grip of the floor. Another way they prevent slipping is to dip their shoes in water and rosin — a sticky substance derived from pine tree sap — right before they go on stage.

Ballerinas also have to break in each pair of toe shoes before they are worn on stage. They have different methods for preparing their unworn shoes so that they are comfortable, flexible, and molded to their feet. Some slam doors on them, throw them against a wall, or bang the toes against the floor. Others break the arches, tear out the inner soles and linings, or squeeze the boxes by hand until they become more supple. If the shoe is tight, it can be stretched by dipping it in alcohol, then remolded on the dancer's foot. It may seem strange that dancers would want to soften up their shoes after cobblers have gone to so much trouble to stiffen them. But most dancers prefer soft shoes — they give less support to the foot but are quieter on stage.

Although pointe shoes are expensive, they have a short life — a pair may last for only one performance. They are then used for class or rehearsal or are given to student dancers. In a multi-act ballet such as *Swan Lake* or *The Sleeping Beauty*, the ballerina dancing the title role may go through two or three pairs of toe shoes each performance.

## Chapter 12

# Servants of the Czar

Nineteenth-century Russia was a vast empire covering one sixth of the globe. A land of both great wealth and appalling poverty, it stretched 6,800 miles from border to border. Although it was a closed autocratic society that discouraged outsiders, it looked to Western Europe, especially France, for its cultural direction. Russia's "Window on Europe" was its elegant capital city, St. Petersburg. Here the pomp and ceremony of the czar's Winter Palace rivaled the splendors of Louis XIV's Versailles, and the broad thoroughfares lined with churches, theaters, and cafes echoed the wide Parisian boulevards.

The story of ballet in Russia begins in 1734, when the Empress Anna invited Jean-Baptiste Landé, a French dancer and ballet master, to St. Petersburg to teach deportment and dancing to the cadets of the Military School for Nobles. Four years later, she allowed him to start the country's first ballet academy to teach social and theatrical dancing. In 1766, Catherine the Great established the Directorate of the Imperial Theatres, in charge of opera, drama, and ballet performances in St. Petersburg and Moscow.

Landé was just the first in a long line of French and Italian ballet masters and dancers who came to Russia. Charles Didelot arrived in 1801 and reorganized the entire teaching system of the Imperial Ballet School. He was followed by Jules Perrot (from 1848 to 1858) and Arthur Saint-Léon (from 1859 to 1870).

All the great Romantic ballerinas — Taglioni, Grahn, Elssler, Grisi, and Cerrito — visited Russia and had great success there. Taglioni was fond of telling of her adventure while on her Russian tour. One night her carriage was stopped by bandits on a lonely forest road. But even they recognized the famous ballerina. Their chief politely told her she could keep her jewels if she would perform for them. Rugs were laid over the mud, and for a quarter of an hour, Taglioni danced. She later claimed, "I never had such an appreciative audience either before or afterwards." After 1850, when serious ballet began to decline in the West, foreign dancers continued to flock to Russia, lured by audiences who appreciated and respected their talents and skills.

The heart of ballet in St. Petersburg was the Maryinsky Theatre and its associated ballet school. Both were under the patronage of the czar, who provided the funds — a million gold rubles a year — for the operation of these institutions and similar ones in Moscow. The Imperial Ballet reflected the hierarchy of the imperial court. The prima ballerina, like the czar, reigned supreme, followed by the other ballerinas, the soloists, and finally, the members of the corps de ballet. Everyone involved with the theaters and the schools — from the ballerinas to the youngest students, the musicians to the stage hands — were considered servants of the czar. When dancers retired, they could become teachers at the Imperial School and were assured of a pension from the state.

Ballet dancing in Russia was a respected profession for both women and men. Students gained admission to the school between the ages of nine and eleven, after interviews and stringent physical examinations, including one to see if they had the proper body proportions. They were expected to devote their lives to the dance. Once selected, they received nine years of meticulous and strenuous ballet training as well as instruction in languages, music, and history.

Students, who sometimes appeared in productions at the Maryinsky, lived at the Theatre Street School at the crown's expense. Discipline was strict. They were considered the equivalent of naval or military cadets. When not in ballet class, the boys wore uniforms; instead of anchors or crossed swords, their collar insignia was Apollo's lyre. The girls wore modest dresses with white aprons. Students had to sign contracts saying they would dance professionally for at least ten years, and upon graduation, they received a gold watch from the czar, which gave them immunity from arrest.

Attending the ballet was a favorite entertainment of the czar, the nobility, the diplomatic corps, the prominent merchants and bankers, and the military elite. The right to coveted boxes and orchestra seats was passed down from father to son. This was an audience that looked on an evening at the Maryinsky as something that would take their minds off of the weighty affairs of state or business that occupied their days. They preferred long ballets that were happy and carefree or full of melodrama. And of course, everything had to be elaborately staged. The general public could also attend performances, but their seats were in the far reaches of the balcony.

St. Petersburg's Maryinsky Theatre (which would become the home of the Kirov Ballet) was the most magnificent in the world — its spacious lobbies filled with velvet hangings and gilt bas-reliefs, a huge cut-crystal chandelier lighting up the auditorium. Its color scheme of cream, gold, and peacock blue was a perfect backdrop for the glamorous, elegantly dressed audience. It was on the Maryinsky stage that ballet would once again be reborn as a great theatrical art. The person considered most responsible was yet another French ballet master, Marius Petipa.

## Chapter 13

# Petipa and the Flowering of Russian Ballet

arius Petipa (1822–1910) came from a four-generation theatrical family. His mother and sister were actresses, and his father was a teacher and choreographer. His older brother, Lucien, also a choreographer, gained fame at the Paris Opera, first as premier danseur and Marie Taglioni's partner, then as ballet master.

As a youth, Marius traveled with his family throughout Europe and even, in 1839, to New York City. He made his dancing debut at the age of sixteen. He eventually partnered both Fanny Elssler and Carlotta Grisi, but even at an early age, he preferred choreographing.

On a hot summer day in 1847, Petipa, just twenty-five, first set foot in St. Petersburg, the city that would be his home for the next sixty years. His brother had arranged for him to dance in his place for one season. His father was already in the city, a teacher at the Imperial Ballet School. Within a few years, Marius was made Soloist to the Czar, married a young Russian ballerina, and became the assistant to ballet master Jules Perrot.

Marius Petipa was a patient man. For the next twelve years, he was allowed to choreograph just a few short dances. In 1862, he finally got his chance to show off his theatrical and choreographic skills. A new evening-length ballet was needed for a guest ballerina's benefit gala. Ballet master Saint-Léon had already left for his summer engagement at the Paris Opera. Petipa, who probably had been preparing for just such an eventuality for a long time, said he could create the necessary five-act ballet in the six weeks that remained until the gala.

Taking his inspiration from excavations then going on near the Egyptian pyramids and a novel by Gautier called *The Romance of the Mummy,* he produced a monumental, four-hour melodramatic ballet called *The Daughter of the Pharaoh.* The cast of four hundred presented scenes at the pharaoh's palace and inside a royal tomb. There was a sword dance, an escape from a lion, and an opium-induced dream scene. In the divertissement, characters representing the world's great rivers presented the national dances of their respective countries. *The Daughter of the Pharaoh* was an immense success, its color and pageantry perfectly suited to the extravagant tastes of the aristocratic audience. When Saint-Léon left Russia for good in 1870, Petipa became ballet-master-in-chief of the Imperial Theatres.

Petipa's ballets were choreographed in the classical style based on the steps, movements, and dance structure of the *ballet d'école.* A typical Petipa ballet was a lavish spectacle of four or five acts and many scenes. It had a romantic or storybook plot told through mime and dance.

Petipa had a gift for combining the basic steps of ballet into almost endlessly innovative patterns that made each dance seem new and different. He choreographed many beautiful passages of pure dance: solos, pas de deux, pas de trois, ensembles for the corps in which "waves" of dancers waltzed across the stage or formed pretty tableaus.

Character dances, ethnic dances, and regal processions were also part of a Petipa evening. He would fill the stage with massive groupings that often included children. He loved using trapdoors, lifts, moving panoramas, and props. His ballets always featured a divertissement, usually in the last act, in the form of a suite of dances not

The corps de ballet of American Ballet Theatre in
Natalia Makarova's restaging of the Kingdom of the
Shades act from *La Bayadère*. The ballet was originally
choreographed by Marius Petipa in 1877 for the
Maryinsky Theatre.

directly related to the plot but meant to display pure dancing.

The highlight of the evening was a grand pas de deux for the
ballerina and her cavalier. These pas de deux followed specific
guidelines that are still used today for classical duets. There are four
musical sections. The first part of the duet is a slow, tender adagio, in
which the man presents and shows off the woman. Then come two
solo variations, one for the danseur, one for the ballerina, in which
they compete in virtuosity. Finally there is the coda, where both

dancers display their allegro technique with a whirlwind of steps and turns moving diagonally across the stage.

Petipa created many such ballets during the 1870s and 1880s. One, *La Bayadère* (1877) contains a famous vision scene set in the Kingdom of the Shades, which harks back to the ghostly second acts of *La Sylphide* and *Giselle.* As the scene opens, the corps, clad in identical white tutus, slowly enters, one by one, down a concealed ramp at the back of the stage. As the dancers appear, each performs the same steps in a hypnotic, breathtaking pattern that is repeated until all thirty-six dancers are arrayed across the stage.

Despite Petipa's seemingly inexhaustible supply of inventive choreography, the public's interest in ballet began to wane. Audiences were becoming bored with long, leisurely ballets fueled by incoherent plots and accompanied by lackluster music. Petipa was in danger of losing his position at the Imperial Theatres. However, several events in the early 1880s would change the course of Russian ballet. It would soon enter a new and splendid era in which Russia became synonymous with ballet, a linkage that would last well into the twentieth century.

## Chapter 14

# The Sleeping Beauty

Russia, despite the quality of its homegrown artists, had always welcomed foreign ballerinas. Beginning in the middle of the nineteenth century, vigorous Italian dancers from Carlo Blasis's Milanese school danced in St. Petersburg and Moscow. In 1885, a magnetic Italian dancer, Virginia Zucchi, made her debut at a summer garden theater in St. Petersburg. Her steely sharp technique thrilled audiences in the capital city. At one performance, a Russian prince actually showered her with diamonds. The influx of Italian ballerinas and their flashy footwork led to a change in the design of the tutu. The mid-calf Romantic skirt became much shorter, made with many layers of net and tarlatan, a thin, stiffened muslin. The skirt stood away from the body, showing off the entire leg. This became known as the classical tutu.

Petipa realized that this dazzling Italian style could help reinvigorate Russian ballet and bring audiences back into the theaters. Enrico Cecchetti (1850–1928), a brilliant Italian dancer and teacher who had studied with Blasis, was invited to come to the Imperial School. There he joined Christian Johannsen, a pupil of Bournonville, who added elements of the Danish style to the dance curriculum, which had emphasized the softer elegance of French *ballet d'école*. This was the beginning of what is called the Russian School of Ballet — a combination of the noble, graceful French style with the more acrobatic, technical brilliance of the Italians.

Ivan Vsevolojsky, the newly appointed director of the Imperial Theatres, involved himself with all aspects of theatrical production, from writing the libretto to designing the costumes. He believed in sparing no expense for costumes and scenery, for he looked on ballet as the equivalent of the court festivities of Louis XIV and Marie Antoinette. In 1888, he decided to give Petipa one last chance to prove himself able to recapture the interest of an apathetic public grown bored with ballet.

Vsevolojsky chose a well-known story from Perrault's 1697 *Mother Goose Tales* — "*La Belle au Bois Dormant*" ("The Sleeping Beauty") — as the subject for Petipa's next ballet. First the director persuaded the great composer Peter Ilyich Tchaikovsky (1840–1893) to write again for the ballet. Vsevolojsky told Tchaikovsky that he had been thinking of writing a libretto based on "The Sleeping Beauty." He envisioned a lavish production in the resplendent Baroque manner of the Sun King, a court ballet that would symbolize the majesty and glory of the czar. He saw *The Sleeping Beauty* as more than a fairy tale about a young girl at the threshold of adulthood. He felt it depicted a struggle between good and evil, which ends with the triumph of love over all odds. It was Vsevolojsky who called the unnamed princess in the original story Aurora, the name of the goddess of dawn. He also named the Lilac Fairy — that flower's lavender color is associated with wisdom in Russian folklore.

Tchaikovsky thought the story a charming one for a ballet and responded enthusiastically to the commission. He wrote to Vsevolojsky:

> *I beseech you to set up a meeting for me with Petipa, in order to work out the details relating to the composition of the music to your libretto. Thinking about this work brings me joy.*

Tchaikovsky was referring to Petipa's unusual way of choreographing. Petipa carefully prepared a scene-by-scene outline, describing the stage action of the ballet, frequently creating the dances before he had a score. He worked out the choreography at home, not in the studio, using diagrams and small figures resembling chess pieces. He then presented the composer with precise, detailed notes, which included explicit instructions about the number and length of the danced and mimed passages, the style of the music, the tempos, the rhythms, and even what instruments to use. One of his more than one hundred instructions to Tchaikovsky for *The Sleeping Beauty* reads:

*Suddenly Aurora notices the old woman who beats on her knitting needles in ²/₄ measures. Gradually she changes to a very melodious waltz in ³/₄, but then suddenly a rest. Aurora pricks her finger. Screams. Pain. Blood streams — give 8 measures in ⁴/₄.*

Tchaikovsky's genius turned Petipa's strict commands into a flowing symphonic score that is visually evocative and filled with rich melodies. Some say it is the finest ballet score ever written, and the composer himself considered it "probably one of my best compositions." Tchaikovsky had studied Adam's score for *Giselle* (his favorite ballet), and he incorporated leitmotivs for Aurora, the good Lilac Fairy, and the evil fairy Carabosse, as well as distinctive music for all the fairies and the divertissement characters.

*The Sleeping Beauty* premiered at the Maryinsky Theatre on January 15, 1890. The principals were the best Italian and Russian dancers of the day. The effervescent and curvaceous Carlotta Brianza, from Milan, was Aurora. Prince Désiré was portrayed by the Imperial Ballet's most gifted danseur, Pavel Gerdt. Petipa's daughter, Marie, was the Lilac Fairy, and Enrico Cecchetti took two very different roles — the hideous Carabosse and the handsome Bluebird in the final act divertissement. The costumes, decor, and scenery were

Carlotta Brianza, the first Aurora in Marius Petipa's 1890 *The Sleeping Beauty.*

among the most lavish that a stage had ever seen; they cost one fourth of the Maryinsky Theatre's entire yearly budget.

The three collaborators, Petipa, Tchaikovsky, and Vsevolojsky, had good reason to be anxious before the curtain rose that premiere night over one hundred years ago. The dress rehearsal a week earlier, presented for the czar, his family and retinue, and influential journalists, had not been well received. Some newspaper critics didn't understand the music; others thought it trivial. The czar's reaction had been even more disheartening. The composer recorded the czar's brief and chilly verbal comment in his diary: " 'Very nice.' His majesty treated me very haughtily. God bless him."

Nonetheless the audiences that flocked to the theater were enthralled. The ballet sold out night after night. Eventually even the critics were convinced of the ballet's worth. "A pearl of great price," one called it.

Petipa's choreography was inspired and fresh, combining all he had learned about grace, elegance, and mime from Perrot, Saint-Léon, and the French School with vigorous elements such as steely pointe work, strong balances, soaring leaps, and multiple turns, which he had garnered from the virtuoso dancers of the Italian School.

The Prologue contains a series of sparkling and distinctive solos as the good fairies bestow their christening gifts on Princess Aurora. Act I, Aurora's sixteenth birthday party, contains the famous "Rose Adagio," an elegant *pas d'action* representing Aurora's coming of age. Technically, this adagio is a study of the pose called attitude. The ballerina, briefly supported by four cavaliers as each ceremoniously presents her with a rose, must sustain difficult balances with seemingly effortless grace.

Act II contains a scene reminiscent of the Romantic ballets of an earlier era. In a forest far from the sleeping princess's palace, the Lilac Fairy shows Prince Désiré, yearning for an ideal love, a dreamlike vision of Aurora, which he pursues among a corps of nymphs.

Act III features the divertissement performed by the fairy tale characters come as guests to the wedding, including a playful, flirtatious duet for a pawing and preening White Cat and Puss in Boots, a reenactment of Little Red Riding Hood's encounter with the Wolf, and a dazzling pas de deux for the Enchanted Princess and the Bluebird. Finally, Aurora and her prince dance a gracious and formal grand pas de deux that reflects their mature love.

Though it was lavish and spectacular, *The Sleeping Beauty* was different from the ballet extravaganzas then being staged. It set a new standard for classical ballet in Russia. Tchaikovsky's music was not just a series of unrelated tunes strung together. The score, complete in itself, is intensely visual and helps tell the story. Vsevolojsky and Petipa's libretto is logical; each scene has a continuity that leads into the next scene. The decor and costumes had a unity of style. Unlike other ballets of the period, in which different designers — often with clashing ideas — designed different acts, *The Sleeping Beauty* was designed by one person. In his choreography, Petipa combined academic style with a high level of technique in a summation of eighteenth- and nineteenth-century ballet — court dances and processions from the eighteenth century, a *ballet blanc* from the Romantic age, and bravura skills from his own time. *The Sleeping Beauty* would not be seen outside of Russia for thirty-one years. Western Europe's first glimpse of this masterpiece would influence and change the history of ballet.

Petipa was nearly seventy when he created *The Sleeping Beauty*. Before him still lay work on two more great ballets that would define forever the great era of classical Russian ballet.

## *Mime in Ballet*

Pantomime, or mime — acting without words, speech translated into movement — is one of the oldest forms of theater and can be found in theatrical traditions all around the world.

The pantomime tradition in ballet goes back to Renaissance court entertainments and masques. It was also influenced by the commedia dell'arte, a form of traveling street theater that arose in Italy in the mid–sixteenth century and became popular all across Europe. Even before Noverre stressed the importance of combining dance and dramatic gesture in ballet, an English dancing master named John Weaver was producing mimed plays and ballets at London's Drury Lane

Theatre. His *The Loves of Mars and Venus* (1717) is the first recorded dance entertainment that told its story without song or speech.

Pantomime was an important feature of ballets in the nineteenth century, and all the great dancers of the time were accomplished at using gestures to convey meaning, feeling, and action. The exceptional story ballets of the period — *La Sylphide, Giselle, The Sleeping Beauty, Swan Lake, The Nutcracker, La Bayadère* — employed a special language of mime and gestures that is still used today.

*Anger:* shake fists above the head.

*Ask:* clasp the hands together in a pleading, imploring gesture.

*Beautiful:* with the right hand held so the thumb is near the face, make a circle around the face from the right to the left.

*Dancing:* raise arms high above head with the hands circling each other.

*Death:* cross outstretched wrists, with fists tightly clenched, in front of the body.

*Fear:* hold hands in front of body, with palms facing outward, while leaning the upper body backward or turning away from the danger; raise left arm over the head, shielding the face with right palm.

*Love:* place crossed hands over the heart, the head turned slightly to the left.

*Marriage:* use the right index finger to point to the ring finger on the other hand.

*Money:* imitate the counting of money between the thumb and the third finger into the other hand below.

*Obey:* point to floor with a strong gesture.

*Remember:* touch temple with index finger.

*Sad:* fingers trace tears falling down the face.

*See:* place a hand or finger by the eye.

*Shoot:* raise the arms as though aiming a bow and arrow.

## Chapter 15

# A Nutcracker Prince and a Swan Queen

Vsevolojsky wanted to follow up quickly on the success of *The Sleeping Beauty* with another Petipa-Tchaikovsky collaboration. The new ballet would share a double bill with a Tchaikovsky one-act opera. For his libretto, Vsevolojsky turned to E. T. A. Hoffmann's *The Nutcracker and the Mouse King,* as adapted by the French novelist Alexandre Dumas. The original story contained macabre scenes and visions of terror. Vsevolojsky softened the more grotesque elements and set Act I of *The Nutcracker* at a children's Christmas party and Act II in a fantasy Land of Sweets. This ballet is a child's world of dreams and enchantments: a young girl's toy nutcracker is really a prince in disguise; toy soldiers are victorious over an army of mice; a walnut-shell boat carries the young hero and heroine through a blizzard to a magical kingdom of sugar plums, candy, and flowers.

As was his usual custom, Petipa provided a detailed scenario for the ballet accompanied by equally detailed musical instructions for the composer. Tchaikovsky initially thought that the first act setting was too mundane for a fairy tale ballet. He also believed it would be "impossible to portray the Sugar Plum Kingdom" and confided to a friend that the images from a land of sweets "do not cheer me or bring me inspiration but haunt me while awake and asleep." He eventually came to like the story, however, and occasionally acted as rehearsal pianist.

The snowflake corps de ballet in the first *Nutcracker* (1892).

As rehearsals for the ballet began, Petipa took ill. The job of staging the ballet fell to Petipa's assistant of many years, Lev Ivanov, who followed the ballet master's written scenario but contributed his own choreography.

Russian-born Ivanov (1834–1901) was a charming and modest man who had spent his entire career under the shadow of Petipa. He loved music and was an accomplished pianist. He was less interested in technical virtuosity, believing that choreography should be an interpretation of the score, the movements stemming directly from the music, not the other way around. Ballet, he said, should be the "blossoming of music." Unlike Petipa, he had to hear the music before he could devise a step.

Ivanov had a particular talent for creating exquisite dances for the corps de ballet. For Act I of *The Nutcracker*, he choreographed a "Waltz of the Snowflakes," a dance in 3/4 time for sixty women in white tutus who whirl and circle in patterns of stars and snowballs. Act II contains the famous "Waltz of the Flowers," in which the dancers' movements imitate the opening and closing of petals, as well as a suite of dances for coffee, tea, chocolate, marzipan, ginger, and candy canes.

*The Nutcracker* premiered at the Maryinsky Theatre on December 17, 1892. Despite a lavish production that included a cast of two hundred, the ballet was not initially a success. It was performed only eleven times before it was dropped from the repertoire. Again, the critics didn't understand Tchaikovsky's witty and sparkling music. They thought the story unsophisticated. They didn't like Ivanov's choreography, and they were particularly cruel to the plump Italian ballerina who danced the Sugar Plum Fairy the first night, implying that she had overindulged in the Land of Sweets before coming on stage. The czar thought the staging "superb," but it seems you can never please a czar, for he added that it might be "too magnificent — the eye gets tired of so much gorgeousness."

More than a decade would pass before the ballet was performed again. It wasn't until the early years of the new century that *The Nutcracker* won over the Russian public, but it soon became a Christmas tradition at the Maryinsky. Although Tchaikovsky's suite of dances from the ballet was a popular concert piece in Europe and America for many years, the whole ballet was not seen in England until 1934 and was not performed in the United States for another ten years. Today, *The Nutcracker,* in hundreds of different choreographic versions, is perhaps the most performed classical ballet in the world, a magical holiday present for children and adults alike.

## The Waltz

In the early nineteenth century, a dance craze swept Europe. Although first denounced as immoral, it soon became the most common social dance on the continent and has remained in the repertoire of ballroom dancers to this day. Its gay melodies and triple-time rhythms affected composers of both popular and serious music, and ballet choreographers have incorporated its steps and movements into the classical vocabulary. That dance is the waltz.

The waltz was popular with all levels of society — parlor maids and princesses, servants and shopkeepers, clerks and countesses. Unlike the stately gavotte and minuet, the most popular social dances of the previous century, the waltz, with its lively tempos, freed dancers to create their own patterns as they swept across the floor.

The waltz started out as a popular country dance in which men and women danced in close embrace. Its ancestors were the sixteenth-century volta and the seventeenth-century *drehtanze*, or twirling dance, in which couples also danced face to face rather than side by side or a discreet distance apart. By the middle of the eighteenth century, modified versions of the waltz had infiltrated aristocratic ballrooms like breaths of fresh country air. By the turn of the century, it had twirled its way into the drawing rooms of the growing middle class.

The waltz was a subject of controversy from the beginning because it was the first dance that allowed a gentleman to put his arms around a lady in public. In the late eighteenth century, dancing masters thought the waltz might injure the mind; in the early nineteenth century, it was called a "wicked, wicked" dance and was condemned by the clergy as "the rhythmic incantation of the Devil." In 1816, an editorial appeared in the *London Times* attacking the dance because

> *the voluptuous intertwining of the limbs, and the close composure of their bodies . . . is indeed far removed from the modest reserve which has hitherto been considered distinctive of English females. . . . We feel it is a duty to warn every parent against exposing their daughters to so fatal a contagion. . . . We trust it will never again be tolerated by any moral society.*

But the indignation of the *Times* fell on deaf ears. The waltz became even more popular over the years, not only in England but in the United States as well. Vienna, Austria, however, was the waltz capital of the world, the home of many public dance palaces, including a great hall that could accommodate three thousand whirling couples at one time.

Ballet and the waltz were made for each other. Its lively tempos and flowing, sweeping movements have intrigued choreographers for many years. The classical, evening-long ballets of the nineteenth century — *Giselle, The Sleeping Beauty, Swan Lake, Raymonda, La Bayadère, The Nutcracker* — all contain waltzes for large ensembles. In modern ballets, waltzes are often used for pas de deux.

*Swan Lake*, the last of the great Tchaikovsky-Petipa-Ivanov ballets, was actually the composer's first ballet score. In 1875, he had received a commission from the Moscow Imperial Theatre (now called the Bolshoi Ballet). He was paid eight hundred rubles for a new ballet, a sum that was nearly half of what he earned during a whole year teaching at the Conservatory.

Tchaikovsky, who thought that ballet was "the most innocent, the most moral of all the arts," suggested the libretto for *Swan Lake*. Years earlier, for a family entertainment, he had composed a short ballet based on a Russian fairy tale about a wicked sorcerer who turns young girls into birds. He expanded this story into *Swan Lake*, a moving ballet of romance and tragedy. Enchanted by sorcerer Von Rothbart, Odette, the Swan Queen, assumes her human form only between the hours of midnight and dawn. It will take the pledge of eternal love by a man who has forsaken all other women to break this spell. Prince Siegfried falls in love with Odette but is tricked into proposing marriage to Von Rothbart's daughter, Odile. Although his betrayal seals the Swan Queen's fate, she forgives him. The lovers triumph over the evil magician by throwing themselves into the lake — their self-sacrificing love frees the Swan Maidens from the curse and destroys Von Rothbart's power forever.

The first performance of *Swan Lake* took place in Moscow in 1877, and it was a dismal failure. The staging was done by an uninspired choreographer whose work was dull and routine. The conductor didn't like the music, and the ballerina who was to play Odette had declared that the score was too difficult to dance to, so she felt free to insert her favorite music and choreography from other ballets. *Swan Lake* was soon dropped from the repertoire, and Tchaikovsky, who blamed his music for the failure, would not write for the ballet for another twelve years.

Tchaikovsky died in 1893. He was by then a respected composer whose achievements were hailed around the world. He had also done more than any other composer to elevate the quality of ballet music in the nineteenth century, making it the equal partner of the choreography. For a special memorial service honoring him, Vsevolojsky and Petipa, who knew just how wonderful the *Swan Lake* score really was, wanted to revive the ballet in a new production. There was, however, only enough time to prepare one act. Once again, Petipa fell ill, and Lev Ivanov was given the task of choreographing *The Flight of Swans*, the lakeside scene in which Prince Siegfried first encounters Odette. Czar Nicholas II was so impressed that he ordered the entire four-act ballet to be produced, specifying that Ivanov's choreography was to be kept for Act II and an added Act IV. Petipa would stage Acts I and III, set at the prince's court.

The new *Swan Lake* premiered on January 27, 1895. It was easy to see that the ballet had been choreographed by two people with different ideas about dance, but this did nothing to detract from the ballet's beauty and magic. Ivanov used his interpretation of Tchaikovsky's music to extend the dramatic potential of the academic style. He created inspired lyrical dances filled with emotion for the Swan Queen and the corps of Swan Maidens. He gave Odette fluttering winglike arm and hand movements, tremulous foot beats, and preening gestures — she was truly a woman trapped in the body of a bird. He used the ballerina's technical skill and arching arabesques to convey the yearning love of the Swan Queen for the prince. Ivanov's two lakeside scenes have a dramatic intensity and magical grace that links them to the *ballets blancs* of the Romantic era, but his corps is an active and animated ensemble that interacts with the soloists.

Petipa's acts, set in the real world of a royal court, contrast sharply with the emotional, poetic passages for the swans. Here, the choreography follows the standard formula for Russian ballets of the period. The story is told through alternating scenes of mime and dancing, and the choreography includes brilliant solos, duets, trios, national dances (Spanish, Hungarian, Neapolitan, and Polish), and divertissements.

The first Swan Queen was Pierina Legnani (1863–1923), an Italian *prima ballerina assoluta* (a title awarded in Russia only to the very best ballerinas). She had made her Russian debut two years earlier, amazing the audience with a technical feat they had never seen before. Legnani was the first ballerina to execute a series of thirty-two consecutive fouettés. She had amazing strength and could remain steadily in one place on one leg while performing these whipped turns. Understandably, Legnani was protective of the secret that allowed her to do those multiple turns without getting dizzy, and she would not allow anyone to see her practicing them. A Russian ballerina, Mathilde Kchessinska, solved the mystery by hiding in the wings during a rehearsal. Legnani was spotting — focusing on a specific fixed object while spinning in her pirouettes. During each turn, she looked for as long as possible at that fixed point before snapping her head around to look at that object again.

Petipa knew a crowd pleaser when he saw one, so he inserted

the thirty-two fouettés into the third act "Black Swan" pas de deux in which the prince, thinking that Odile is Odette, proclaims his love for the evil imposter.

The dual role of Odette-Odile is considered one of the most challenging in the ballerina's repertoire, not only because of its technical difficulty but because the dancer must, in alternate acts, display both purity and evil with equal skill.

*Swan Lake* was the last of the great nineteenth-century Russian ballets. New works were produced at the Maryinsky, but none could match that collaboration in emotional intensity, inventive choreography, and glorious music.

A new century was dawning. Tchaikovsky and Ivanov were dead, and a new director had succeeded Vsevolojsky. The new director did not like Petipa, who he thought was too old and too set in his ways. Petipa's last ballet, *The Magic Looking-Glass* (1903), was a disaster that was booed and hissed at the premiere. His contract was not renewed, and cruelly, he was forbidden backstage entrance at the theater where he had faithfully served four czars for six decades. Petipa died in 1910, a bitter old man dreaming of the glories that once were.

The legacy left by Petipa was impressive. He had choreographed forty-six new ballets and collaborated on or revised seventeen more. He had overseen the creation of the Russian School of Ballet, fusing French grace and elegance with Italian fire and brilliance. He had shaped the Imperial Ballet into a glorious crown jewel of classical style, virtuosic technique, and musical quality — another Golden Age.

# Part IV

# The Twentieth Century

Dancers from the New York City Ballet in George
Balanchine's *Square Dance,* choreographed in 1957.

between green
                    mountains
sings the flinger
of

fire     beyond red rivers
of fair perpetual
feet the
sinuous

                    riot

the
flashing
bacchant.

partedpetaled
mouth, face
delirious. indivisible
grace

          of dancing

— e. e. cummings

## Chapter 16

# The Rebel

The closing years of the nineteenth century and the early years of the twentieth were relatively peaceful ones on the European continent. Alliances between the great nations kept an uneasy balance of power, even as their armies were secretly preparing for war. Great Britain, France, Germany, Italy, and Belgium were busy expanding their colonial empires in Africa, the Middle East, and Asia. For the very rich it was an age of opulence, for the middle class a prosperous and comfortable time. Living conditions even improved some for workers and the poor.

Although it was a time of peace and prosperity, the new century brought stirrings of artistic and political reform and revolution. Some writers and painters in England, Western Europe, and America were beginning to question the prim, proper, often overly sentimental attitudes that had characterized the Victorian age. A new social consciousness and compassion for the oppressed and downtrodden was emerging. Art and literature experienced a trend toward expression and emotion. Artists no longer imitated nature exactly; instead they transformed or distorted what they saw. The world might appear to be carefree and sunny, but some painters and writers wanted to explore the harsher and darker realities that lurked beneath the surface of things. Like most progressive movements in the arts, these modern ideas and styles exasperated the critics and public alike, who thought the new works ugly and insulting.

Czarist Russia, too, at this time, was feeling stirrings of political and artistic change, which would soon affect the ballet world. Economically the country was trying to catch up to the West by modernizing its industries and transportation systems. In 1905, a series of often bloody peasant uprisings, worker strikes, and military mutinies led Czar Nicholas II to issue a constitution. An elected parliamentary government was established. Complete autocratic rule by the czar was abolished, but other social changes were slow in coming. The feeling of rebellion, revolution, and the need to change the established order of things even found its way into the stately halls of the tradition-bound Maryinsky Theatre.

In St. Petersburg in the early 1900s, a brilliant young dancer, Michel Fokine (1880–1942) was questioning some long-held and basic assumptions about ballet. Fokine was intelligent, a fine musician, artist, and actor who was well on his way to becoming a star at the Maryinsky. But he was also an activist and a rebel. Inspired by the 1905 workers' revolt, he and ballerina Anna Pavlova had led a short-lived and unsuccessful dancers' strike for better working conditions and higher salaries. They also wanted dancers to have more of a say in the running of the Imperial Theatres. And they demanded that the order keeping Petipa from visiting backstage be rescinded. It was only Fokine's and Pavlova's great popularity with the public that kept them from being fired by the Maryinsky director when the strike was broken.

Fokine had a vision of ballet and theatrical dance that was strikingly different from the prevailing views. He had studied Noverre's *Letters* and wanted to update the eighteenth-century reformer's ideas, bringing them into the modern age. He had also been influenced by seeing Isadora Duncan. In 1904, she had brought her revolutionary form of expressive dance to Russia. It was a liberating experience for Fokine to see the American, clad in loose, revealing draperies, with bare feet and flowing hair, dance with such freedom. Even the music she used was radical for a dancer — Beethoven, Wagner, Chopin.

As early as 1904, Fokine had sent memos to the administration at the Maryinsky, pressing them to expand the possibilities of classical ballet by opening it up to a new expressiveness, poetry, and freedom of movement. Ballet in Russia, Fokine felt, was just a pleasant way of passing an evening; it no longer touched the emotions of the audience. Fokine wanted to replace the long, rambling, often incoherent ballets, which were all choreographed to the same formula and all danced in the same type of costume. Instead he wanted tightly knit stories on a single theme, danced with expressive intensity, artistic consistency, and historical accuracy. He wanted ballet once again to be a serious art.

Fokine thought dancers should dance with their entire body, using their arms, torsos, and heads, as well as their legs, to communicate meaning. In his new ballet, expressive movements and natural gestures, appropriate to the scenario's historical period, would be used to convey character, emotion, and the spirit and story of the ballet. The corps would not be merely decorative but should play an integrated part. Ballet music should be of the highest quality, which meant using compositions and serious symphonic works previously thought unsuitable for the dance. Music, Fokine felt, was an organic part of ballet, not just a background of pleasing sounds.

Both costume and decor should relate to the period and theme of the ballet. Tutus and toe shoes might not be appropriate for every work. Ballet dancers might even perform barefoot. Historical accuracy could be reconstructed through a careful study of painting and sculpture. Finally, the choreographer, composer, and artist should work together to produce a work that is a harmonious whole.

Although Fokine was allowed to create a few ballets at the Maryinsky, his ideas were generally ignored by the conservative establishment. He would not be able to put all his reforms into practice until he joined with another young rebel, Serge Diaghilev, in an enterprise that would revolutionize the world of dance and change Western culture.

*Chapter 17*

# The Impresario

The man responsible for the creation of modern classical ballet and its revolutionary rebirth as a serious art was not a dancer, choreographer, musician, or artist. Serge Diaghilev (1879–1929) was an impresario, or director-manager — a man of great charm, taste, and personal magnetism whose gift was the ability to discover new talent and inspire artistic collaboration.

Diaghilev came from a cultured family, members of Russia's minor nobility. He grew up in Perm, a city one thousand miles from the Russian capital. Although he originally wanted to be a composer, he went to St. Petersburg at the age of eighteen to study law. There he joined a group of students who hoped to shake up the stuffy cultural establishment of turn-of-the-century Russia. The group called themselves the New Pickwickians, after characters in a Charles Dickens novel; their leader was an artist named Alexander Benois (1870–1960) whose aristocratic ancestors had fled to Russia to avoid the French Revolution and whose grandfather had designed the Maryinsky Theatre. Benois introduced Diaghilev to the ballet, taking him to see *The Sleeping Beauty.* Another member of the group, designer Léon Bakst (1866–1924), also helped arouse and cultivate Diaghilev's interest in art by taking him to museums and galleries.

Along with other New Pickwickians, Diaghilev founded a magazine in 1899 to expose Russia to the new trends in Western art, from Impressionism to futurism. He had worked briefly as an assistant to the director of the Imperial Theatres, and his dream was to bring the glories, richness, and beauties of Russian art and music to the West. In 1906, Diaghilev organized an exhibition of Russian art in Paris, and in the following years, he presented a successful series of concerts as well as a Russian opera. When he decided in 1909 to add dance to the next four-week "Saison Russe" in Paris, he said, "I had already presented Russian painting, Russian music, and Russian opera in Paris, and from opera to ballet is but a step! Ballet contains in itself all these other activities." That decision was a fateful one for the history of ballet.

Diaghilev gathered around him the best artists from the Imperial Theatres — fifty-five dancers, including ballerina Anna Pavlova (1888–1931), who had already toured Europe to great acclaim, and her rival, Tamara Karsavina (1885–1976), an expressive dancer of great beauty, exquisite delicacy, and riveting acting ability. Also in the troupe was a nineteen-year-old sensation, Vaslav Nijinsky (1889–1950), who would become the first male ballet celebrity of the twentieth century. Nijinsky had a magnetic stage presence. His extraordinary gravity-defying leaps combined with whisper-soft landings created a new image for the danseur, no longer just a partner or porter, but a superstar.

Diaghilev was impressed with Michel Fokine's radical and experimental ideas, and he asked the choreographer to restage several of his ballets. Benois and Bakst would contribute their artistic talents to the enterprise, which would initially be supported by money from rich Russian and French patrons. Music and painting would join the art of dance, making ballet a "total theater."

The Paris Opera would not allow outside troupes to dance on their stage, so Diaghilev refurbished the seedy Châtelet Theater. The cultured Parisian society already knew that Serge Diaghilev would present something new, exciting, and unexpected because of the exhibits and musical productions he had brought from Russia. They waited in anticipation for opening night, May 19, 1909. Ever the showman, Diaghilev made sure that well-known figures from the worlds of theater, art, and music were in the audience. Diaghilev himself was an attraction. An imposingly tall and heavyset figure, he sported a top hat, fur-trimmed coat, a monocle, a mustache, and a flamboyant streak of white in his black-dyed hair.

In the city where Sallé, Camargo, Taglioni, and Elssler had once danced, ballet had become a practically dead art, so the technical virtuosity and exotic boldness of the Russians was electrifying. Fokine's ideas of artistic unity and harmony were an eye-opening experience. Instead of one long evening-length ballet, Diaghilev presented several shorter ballets, each with a separate, consistent, yet distinctly different dancing style, music, theme, and decor. Each piece was meant to evoke strong emotions in the viewers.

Glorifying eighteenth-century French culture, *Le Pavillon d'Armide* brought France's famous Gobelin tapestries to life. In *Prince Igor*, a one-act ballet set to music from the opera of the same name by Russian composer Alexander Borodin, the explosive strength and animal grace of the men stunned an audience that had forgotten the thrilling virtuosity of the virile male dancer. *Les Sylphides*, a suite of dances for sylphs and a melancholy poet, to music by Frédéric Chopin, recaptured the moonlit, dreamlike spirit of the Romantic age. Because there is no story in this ballet, it is sometimes called the first abstract, or plotless, ballet. *Cleopatra*, a dramatic and theatrically spectacular vision of ancient Egypt, included a dazzling and seductive entrance for the Queen of the Nile, who was wrapped like a mummy in brilliantly colored silks.

There was no question that the Russians would return the following spring with more novel and exotic ballets. The debut season had been so memorable that the Paris Opera changed its mind and invited them to perform there in 1910. Diaghilev decided that instead of having Fokine rework older ballets from the Maryinsky repertoire, totally new collaborations should be created.

Diaghilev was always aware that scandal sells tickets. The one-act *Scheherazade*, to music by Nicolai Rimsky-Korsakov, unfolded like a series of three-dimensional paintings, retelling shocking stories from the *Arabian Nights* with all the sensational melodrama of the popular silent films of the day. Léon Bakst's sensual scenery and costumes used bold, bright colors meant to evoke strong emotional reactions from the audience. His unusual range of intense contrasting colors was a design revolution at a time when pale Art Nouveau shades were the fashion. French fashion designers and interior decorators quickly adapted Bakst's stage settings and costumes, bringing an Eastern influence to clothing and home furnishings that lasted for a decade.

Fokine's choreography, based in part on his study of Persian miniature paintings, was filled with sinuous body movements for the women and daring leaps for the half-naked men. The role of the Golden Slave was danced by Nijinsky, in an incredible performance that combined an aura of Eastern mystery with jumps of breathtaking height. Nijinsky claimed that his formula for his fantastic jumps was "just to go up there and pause a little."

Another ballet from that 1910 season, *Firebird*, had even more far-reaching effects on the development of modern ballet, for it marked the beginning of a twenty-year collaboration between Diaghilev and Igor Stravinsky (1882–1971), the greatest musical innovator of the twentieth century. Fokine wanted to do a totally Russian ballet, one based on several Russian *skazki*, or folktales, about an evil wizard, enchanted princesses, and a brave hunter prince who breaks the spell with the help of the magical Firebird. When the composer originally commissioned to write the score was slow in delivering the music, Fokine turned to Stravinsky, a little-known twenty-seven-year-old Russian composer who had helped orchestrate some of the music for *Les Sylphides*.

Stravinsky, collaborating closely with the choreographer and the designer, created a brilliant and inventive score, filled with the mystery, splendor, and fantasy of Russian fairy tales. The music shimmered like the golden embroidery on the sumptuous flame-colored costumes. Although the music was influenced by Russian folk songs and had a traditional structure, it had a modern sense of dynamic movement and energy.

The dancing, which combined classical ballet techniques and freer, more expressive, interpretive styles, was equally as memorable. The role of the Firebird, originally offered to Pavlova (she turned it down because she didn't like the difficult rhythms), was given to Karsavina. Fokine danced the Prince, and Enrico Cecchetti, the company's teacher, was the wizard Kastchei. *Firebird* was a great success, and like a number of the ballets created under the direction of Diaghilev, it is still, in various versions, in the repertoire of many contemporary companies.

Despite several seasons of popular and critical acclaim, Diaghilev's troupe was not a permanent one, for he could only take his dancers to Paris during their vacations; rehearsals had to be fit in whenever time was available from their official duties. Diaghilev wanted to form a permanent group, to be built around the talents of his protégé, Nijinsky. A scandal at the Maryinsky allowed him to do just that. Diaghilev's Ballets Russes, the first great ballet company to exist without the backing of a king, queen, or czar, would become the most exciting creative force in Europe for the next two decades.

Early in 1911, Nijinsky was abruptly dismissed from the Maryinsky, because, it was said, he had shocked the sensibilities of the dowager empress. His crime: dancing in a tunic that she considered to be too short and revealing. The dancer selected by Diaghilev to be the centerpiece of the Ballets Russes was now free, and seasons were planned for Rome, Monte Carlo, and London, as well as Paris.

Two celebrated roles were created that year for Nijinsky. Petrouchka, the soulful, tormented puppet in the ballet of the same name, and the Spirit of the Rose in *Le Spectre de la Rose*. These parts displayed his genius as a dancer and his uncanny ability to transform himself on stage to become any character called for.

Vaslav Nijinsky in his favorite role, the puppet with a human soul, Petrouchka (1911).

*Petrouchka* was a collaborative effort by Fokine, Stravinsky, and Benois. Together, they expanded a Stravinsky piano concerto into a scenario for this ballet about a tragic puppet clown, a Russian Pierrot, who, according to the composer, was "the eternal and unhappy hero of all fairgrounds, and all countries."

The ballet is set in St. Petersburg in the 1830s during the annual winter Shrovetide Fair. Among the festive activities, a darker story is being enacted at the theater booth of the sinister Showman-Magician. He is master of three puppets, who, after the fair is closed for the night, play out their own drama of desire and murder.

Petrouchka suffers jealous torments over his unrequited love for the rosy-cheeked, heartless Ballerina. She in turn is bedazzled by the brutal, self-absorbed Moor, who kills Petrouchka, his rival, in a fit of rage. Although Nijinsky's role called for little virtuoso dancing but rather for jerky steps, rigid movements, and limp postures, it showed off the dancer's brilliant talent for acting and mime. Nijinsky made

Vaslav Nijinsky and Tamara Karsavina in *Le Spectre de la Rose* (1911).

Petrouchka a tragic figure driven by human longings and thwarted desires, a puppet with a soul.

Stravinsky's music was daring and original — so strange that at the first rehearsal the members of the orchestra burst out laughing. The score, which contains fragments of folk tunes and popular songs, is a musical portrait of the fairground activities, the rivalry between the puppets, and Petrouchka's "death."

Fokine highlighted Nijinsky's extraordinary leaps in another ballet in that 1911 season. *Le Spectre de la Rose*, set to Carl Maria von Weber's 1819 work "Invitation to the Dance," was based on a poem by Gautier: "I am the spirit of a rose / That you wore at last night's ball. . . ." A young girl, danced by Karsavina, returns home from her first ball, then falls asleep in a chair, clasping an admirer's rose in her hand. As she dreams about the romance of the evening, Nijinsky, portraying the Spirit of the Rose, suddenly soars through an open window. He waltzes a dreamlike pas de deux with Karsavina that embodies all the freshness and yearning of young love. And then, with another magical jump, he is gone.

Nijinsky's ability as a dancer was unquestioned. Now Diaghilev, who may have begun to think that Fokine's new kind of ballet was not new enough, set out to turn his adored protégé into a choreographer.

# Chapter 18

# "Astonish Me!"

To teach Nijinsky about painting, sculpture, and music, Diaghilev took the young dancer to museums, galleries, and concerts. Because the impresario desired that his company be more daring and provocative with each season, he wanted his protégé to create ballets that were even fresher and more experimental than Fokine's. While vacationing in Greece, Bakst had sketched dancers depicted on antique pottery and on temple friezes. These drawings became the inspiration for Nijinsky's first choreographic effort.

Diaghilev was known to tell artistic collaborators, "Astonish me!" Nijinsky's first choreographic efforts certainly did. His first ballet, *The Afternoon of a Faun (L'Après-Midi d'un Faune)* bore very little relationship or resemblance to Petipa's classical ballet or even to Fokine's more naturalistic choreography. The impressionistic music of Claude Debussy, composed between 1892 and 1894, had originally been used as a musical prelude to the poem by Stéphane Mallarmé after which the ballet is named: "In the heat of a sunny afternoon a Faun lies dreaming of nymphs dancing before him. One is so beautiful he wants to possess her."

Nijinsky's choreography went even further than Fokine's in presenting steps and movements that belonged to the period in which the ballet was set. The dancers, dressed in semitransparent costumes, looked like they had just stepped off an ancient Greek vase or wall painting. The dancers were barefoot or wore sandals. Their

Vaslav Nijinsky as the Faun with his sister, Bronislava Nijinska, as a Nymph in Nijinsky's first choreographic effort, *The Afternoon of a Faun* (1912).

slow, angular movements were done with their heads, arms, and feet in profile, while their bodies were turned toward the audience. The choreography, mostly walking and posing, was a total rejection of the classical ballet vocabulary — there were no high elevations or fluid, graceful movements. Feet were not turned out, and the steps were performed in straight lines in two-dimensional space along a narrow strip of the stage.

Nijinsky had choreographed positions and movements for the entire body, down to the dancers' fingertips. This style was derived, in part, from a system called Eurythmics (literally "good rhythm") developed a few years earlier by Emile Jaques-Dalcroze, a musician and teacher. It was originally devised to teach music students coordination and a sense of rhythm. The dancers found Nijinsky's new steps and poses so alien that it took over one hundred rehearsals to prepare the ballet, which lasts for only eight minutes.

Nijinsky's Faun was a pagan creature, half man, half beast. His final erotic pose, in which he caresses a scarf dropped by the fleeing nymph, was considered by many to be so obscene and scandalous that it was toned down in subsequent performances.

*The Afternoon of a Faun* caused a sensation when it premiered at the Châtelet Theater on May 19, 1912. Some in the audience hissed and booed. Bravely, instead of the usual curtain call, Diaghilev had the short ballet repeated as an encore — and it was then loudly applauded. The French newspapers condemned the ballet as "indecent," "lecherous," and "loathsome," but these reviews made for good ticket sales and gave the company worldwide publicity.

Fokine, who was choreographic director of the company, had been planning his own Greek-style ballet. He was so shocked by Nijinsky's elevation to choreographer and by the work he had produced that he resigned from the company a few months later.

Nijinsky choreographed slowly. *Jeux* (*Games*), to music commissioned from Debussy, premiered the next year. The ballet, in which the dancers were dressed in contemporary tennis clothes, was not a success. It was Nijinsky's third ballet, *The Rite of Spring (Le Sacre du Printemps),* that would shatter old ideas about beauty and grace forever.

The Tribal Maidens from Nijinsky's controversial 1913 ballet, *The Rite of Spring,* danced to Stravinsky's pounding score. Marie Rambert is second from the left.

It was considered by many to be the most shocking artistic event of the age. The work was a collaboration with Igor Stravinsky, who supplied the music and scenario, and Russian painter and archaeologist Nicholas Roerich, who designed the scenery and costumes. The work opened one month after *Jeux*'s premiere, on May 19, 1913.

Nijinsky's vision was astonishing. Stravinsky called it "controlled hysteria." Subtitled *Pictures of Pagan Russia*, the ballet was a powerful depiction of an awe-inspiring prehistoric ritual sacrifice. It included a brutal, frenzied dance for the Chosen One, a young maiden selected by the tribe to dance herself to death in a sacrifice to appease the gods of nature. *The Rite of Spring* was a ballet of the earth, not the air. Dressed in Roerich's costumes, painted in muted browns, beiges, and reds, the dancers moved heavily and adopted awkward, contorted poses: toes and knees bent and pointed in, arms held rigid; heads, inclined toward shoulders, rested on the backs of the hands.

Nijinsky had gone even further than before in developing an entirely new and personal style that was the opposite of the classicism and elevation for which he had been applauded as a dancer. For lightness and grace he substituted heaviness and angularity; instead of open gestures, there were turned-in poses and flat planes. Like the early pioneers of modern dance, Nijinsky was experimenting with new and different ways of moving.

Everyone — audience and dancers alike — was aghast at the primitive brutality of the piece. The dancers, challenged by its difficulty, had required 120 rehearsals. To help Nijinsky teach the complex counts and rhythms, Diaghilev had had to hire a young Polish-born British dancer and teacher, Marie Rambert, who had studied with Jaques-Dalcroze.

Stravinsky's complicated music for *The Rite of Spring* was a total departure from anything this inventive composer had done before, and its harsh, dissonant sound contributed to the audience's unease. The music, scored for an exceptionally large orchestra of over one hundred instruments, is filled with novel and constantly changing rhythms. Quiet passages and brief silences lead into staccato bursts of music. Harsh trills and shrill shrieks from the flutes, woodwinds and brass alternate with throbbing percussions and incessant beats that emphasize the pounding feet of the dancers. The music is powerful and violent; it reverberates with the primitive energy of the tribal culture it is describing. The music was so advanced for its time that one critic claimed it would not be understood for thirty years.

The music and the ballet were a glimpse of the political, social, and cultural upheavals and violence that would soon engulf Europe. In the years leading up to the premiere of *The Rite of Spring*, the climate in Europe had become more unstable. A growing number of provocative artists and writers were creating works meant to make a complacent public sit up and take notice. Economic, territorial, and imperialistic rivalries were simmering among Germany, France, Great Britain, Russia, and Austria-Hungary. A series of small armed conflicts and crises in the Balkans, the Far East, and Africa contributed to the feelings of impending war. Even science and technology were playing their parts. Governments now had at their disposal methods of great destruction — chemical warfare, air power, tanks, machine guns. In June 1914, when a Serbian national assassinated Archduke Ferdinand, the heir to the crown of Austria-Hungary, in Sarajevo, it was almost inevitable that the Great War would follow. World War I (1914–1918) would bring about a total breakdown of the old cultural and political orders. A vast change in accepted values and morals would finally shut the door on the artistic ideals and sensibilities of the nineteenth century.

*The Rite of Spring*'s premiere, at the Champs-Elysées Theater, brought on a near-riot. An eyewitness later recounted:

> *Not many minutes passed before a section of the audience began shouting its indignation; on which the rest retaliated with loud appeals for order. The hubbub soon became deafening; the dancers*

*went on, and so did the orchestra, although scarcely a note of the music could be heard. The shouting continued even during the change of scene . . . and now actual fighting broke out among some of the spectators.*

The noise was so great that a pale Nijinsky, standing on a chair in the wings, had to pound out the rhythms and call out the counts so the dancers, who were on the verge of tears, could continue. Despite this noisy mixed reception of catcalls, boos, cheers, and applause, some people that first night knew they were seeing and hearing a masterpiece.

## Modern Dance

Around the turn of the century, musicians and painters were not the only artists attempting to liberate culture from the cobwebs of the past. Some dancers — mostly women — looked at the state of theatrical dancing, on the opera house stages as well as in variety and vaudeville shows, and did not like what they saw. They questioned whether the formal rules of academic ballet were relevant to contemporary life. They criticized the reliance on fairy tale themes, the overblown staging, the use of banal music, the emphasis on crowd-pleasing acrobatic tricks. They began to experiment with more individual styles of dancing.

Perhaps because the United States did not have a centuries-old tradition of classical ballet, the early pioneers of modern dance were American. Loie Fuller (1862–1928), Isadora Duncan (1878–1927), and Ruth St. Denis (1880–1968) each in her own way sought to make dance freer and more expressive, to inspire audiences to a new awareness both of the world around them and of their own sensations and emotions. They were followed by other gifted dancers, choreographers, and teachers whose work kept the United States at the center of the modern dance movement. Martha Graham (1894–1991) created a revolutionary new dance vocabulary and discipline. Intensely expressive, her system of movement uses the contraction and release of the breath as its motivating force. Former Graham Company members Erick Hawkins (born in 1909), Merce Cunningham (born in 1919), and Paul Taylor (born in 1930) went on to found their own companies and further their own explorations and innovations.

Modern dance began as a revolt against classical ballet, so its basic techniques are markedly different:

| *Classical Ballet* | *Modern Dance* |
| --- | --- |
| Based on accepted steps, movements, and traditions that go back hundreds of years | Methods and choreographic styles are more personal, often springing directly from their creator's own talents and artistic visions; may incorporate everyday movements such as walking, skipping, running, and falling |
| Uses five basic positions of the feet and arms | Builds on modified versions of the ballet positions but also uses as many positions as the choreographer needs or can imagine |
| Uses 90-degree turnout | Uses parallel positions, 45-degree turnout, and variations |
| Upper body held stiff and upright | Upper body loose and fluid |
| Knees are kept straight for most positions involving extensions and elevation; generally bent only for the attitude and plié | Steps are often done with bent knees |

| | |
|---|---|
| Movements are graceful and elegant | Movements may be angular, disjointed, convulsive, or percussive |
| Based on symmetrical patterns and designs that are restful to look at | Sometimes uses asymmetrical patterns and designs, which may be disturbing to look at |
| Airborne; tries to overcome laws of gravity | Acknowledges and uses gravity |
| Dancers wear ballet slippers or toe shoes | Full pointe is rejected; dancers usually perform in bare feet to maintain a closer connection to the floor |

Despite their differences in the past, today ballet and modern dance interact and influence each other. Some modern dance choreographers incorporate ballet's lightness and virtuosity into their works; some contemporary ballet choreographers employ modern dance's broken rhythms, off-center balances, weighty movements, unorthodox gestures, and psychological themes. Contemporary modern dance choreographers have been asked to create for ballet companies, and ballet superstars such as Rudolf Nureyev and Mikhail Baryshnikov have danced with modern dance companies. Baryshnikov has taken this interaction between the two styles one step further. In 1990, he cofounded the White Oak Dance Project, a small touring group of experienced dancers from an eclectic range of backgrounds that presents works by a variety of modern choreographers.

## Chapter 19

# A New Protégé and an Old Ballet

The months following the premiere of *The Rite of Spring* brought several major changes for the Ballets Russes. The company went on their first South American tour, but without Diaghilev. He had had an irrational fear of traveling by sea ever since a fortune-teller had predicted that he would die on water. By the time the ship docked in Argentina, Nijinsky was engaged to Romola de Pulska, a young Hungarian aristocrat traveling with the company. The news of their marriage in Buenos Aires so enraged the impresario that he fired his star.

Not only did Diaghilev now need someone to replace Nijinsky as lead dancer; he also needed to find a new protégé to groom as choreographer. He found someone to fill both these roles in Léonide Massine (1895–1979), a seventeen-year-old from Moscow's Bolshoi Theatre. Massine, trained as an actor as well as a dancer, was a young man of great intelligence, physical beauty, and technical ability. He made a highly praised debut with the Ballets Russes in April 1914, in a role originally intended for Nijinsky. Massine would soon become a skilled choreographer with a theatrical flair, creating comic and witty works that perfectly integrated natural mime, stylized folk dance, and classical technique.

Within a few months, the outbreak of the First World War disrupted the company. Some members were inducted into the army; others were detained in hostile countries. Travel around most of

Europe was out of the question, planned seasons in London and Berlin were cancelled, and other bookings were difficult to obtain.

Diaghilev, along with Bakst, Stravinsky, and Massine, settled in neutral Switzerland to wait out the war. Gathering around him as many members of the company as he could, Diaghilev managed, during the next few years, to have seasons in Switzerland, Spain and Portugal (also neutral countries), South America, and the United States, which had not yet entered into the conflict. Meanwhile, Nijinsky tried to form his own company, but its first season, in an English music hall, was not a success. He was often ill, and when he did dance, it was not with the same fire as before. During the war, he and Romola were interned for two years by the Germans. Through the efforts of the American ambassador, they were finally freed. Diaghilev, under pressure from the Metropolitan Opera, sponsors of the Ballets Russes' American tour, invited Nijinsky to rejoin the company in New York. During this period, Nijinsky completed what would be his last ballet, *Til Eulenspiegel*, based on medieval German legends about a hero-rogue.

Nijinsky's final break with Diaghilev came in Spain in the fall of 1917. Nijinsky was twenty-eight, and although no one could then know it, he had performed in public for the last time. In 1920, Nijinsky, who had displayed evidence of eccentric behavior throughout his life, was diagnosed with schizophrenia. He spent the next thirty years, until his death in London in 1950, in and out of asylums. His dancing career had lasted for just a meteoric ten years, and as a choreographer he had created only four ballets. But like fellow Russian Anna Pavlova, his influence on the history of ballet was far-reaching.

Diaghilev's new protégé, Léonide Massine, began to choreograph during World War I. One of his earliest efforts gave an inkling of his droll style. *Parade* (1917) also marked the Ballets Russes' first collaboration with the leader of Paris's artistic avant-garde, the

Spanish-born painter Pablo Picasso, in his debut as a designer for the stage. This association enhanced Diaghilev's reputation as a supporter and promoter of modern art forms. Over the next ten years, a whole range of modern artists, including Henri Matisse, Georges Braque, André Derain, and Juan Gris, worked with the company.

*Parade* is a circus ballet, a succession of sideshow acts at a Parisian fair. The idea and scenario sprang from Jean Cocteau, a young French poet who had been a member of the Diaghilev circle since 1909. He said he got the inspiration for *Parade* when, home on army leave, he attended a concert where the eccentric French composer Erik Satie had played his oddly entitled composition, "Pieces in the Shape of a Pear." Cocteau quickly arranged to meet the composer, who agreed to write a score for the new ballet.

Picasso designed and painted the scenery and costumes in the radical Cubist style. This was the first theatrical application of the

Pablo Picasso's Cubist costumes for Léonide Massine's *Parade* (1917): the New York Manager, a Dancing Horse, and the Paris Manager.

Cubist approach, which reduced objects into their basic geometric shapes and flat planes, forcing people to look at familiar things in new ways. Cubist artists disregarded perspective and showed their subjects from many different angles at the same time. Picasso's ingenious costume constructions included a ten-foot-high cardboard skyscraper that concealed the dancer portraying the New York Manager and a mustachioed, tailcoated Paris Manager (perhaps meant to be Diaghilev) sporting a walking stick and a long pipe. Massine's choreography also incorporated a Cubist influence, using distorted gestures and movements.

Satie's music was a collage of jazz, ragtime, and noises (the sounds of typewriters, pistol shots, and steamship whistles). *Parade* was so different from everyday reality that the French poet Apollinaire coined a new word — *surreal* — to describe the ballet. Within a few years, the term *surrealism* became associated with a new art and literary movement that fused the actual world with that of dreams and the subconscious.

*Parade*, produced in Paris during the darkest days of the war, was a celebration of popular culture. It included references to silent films, music hall acts, automobiles, and airplanes. It was presented only six or seven times, then became one of the lost Diaghilev ballets not to be seen again for fifty years.

The armistice that ended World War I was signed on June 28, 1919, in Versailles. Able to travel outside of neutral territory once again, the Ballets Russes reassembled in London. However, Diaghilev, who still firmly believed that *ballet* was synonymous with *Russia*, made his international ballerinas and danseurs adopt Russian-sounding names when they joined his company. Three of his top dancers — Lydia Sokolova, Anton Dolin, and Alicia Markova — were really British.

In 1919, to celebrate the end of the war, Massine, only twenty-four, created two ballets that are now considered to be his masterpieces. *La Boutique Fantasque (The Fantastic Toy Shop)* was set to music by Gioacchino Rossini as adapted by Ottorino Respighi; the scenery and costumes were by André Derain. The ballet is set in the 1860s in a toy shop on the French Riviera, where dolls of many nationalities — British, American, French, Polish, Italian — come to life at night.

The second ballet was *The Three-Cornered Hat*. Based on a Spanish novel, it was inspired by the company's wartime stay in Spain, where Massine had studied Spanish dance. He incorporated flamenco and traditional folk dancing into a comic love story about a miller and his wife that was set in a small Andalusian village. Diaghilev commissioned the music from Spanish composer Manuel de Falla. The authentic Spanish flavor of the ballet was echoed in the costumes, inspired by Goya paintings, and the scenery, some of which was hand-colored by the designer, Picasso. In *The Three-Cornered Hat*, Picasso introduced a new simplicity into the designs for the Ballets Russes, different from the ostentatious works created by Bakst. Picasso's sets and costumes used only a few bright colors to evoke sunbaked Spain.

Not having any royal or state patronage, the Ballets Russes depended for its continuing existence on its box office ticket sales. The Ballets Russes also depended on its choreographer to provide novelties season after season. By 1921, Massine had been with the group for seven years and had created twelve ballets. That year he married an English dancer, but unlike Nijinsky, he did not wait for Diaghilev to retaliate with a curt dismissal. Massine quit the Ballets Russes, leaving the impresario without a choreographer for the upcoming London season.

Diaghilev decided that what was needed was a ballet so spectacular that it might run for a thousand performances. He wanted a ballet that would show the world the splendors of a now gone imperial Russia. What better choice than to restage Petipa's masterpiece,

*The Sleeping Beauty*, which had not yet been seen in its entirety in the West. No expense was to be spared for this production, now renamed *The Sleeping Princess*.

An ailing Bakst (who died a few years later) designed the magnificent sets and costumes in a mere six weeks. Stravinsky, a great admirer of Tchaikovsky, was asked to reorchestrate the glorious music. Petipa's choreography was recreated by Nicholas Sergeyev, the former régisseur (the stage manager who restages and rehearses all the ballets in a company's repertoire) of the Maryinsky, who had escaped the 1917 Russian Revolution with all his notes intact. Bronislava Nijinska, Nijinsky's sister, contributed some new sections to the last act wedding divertissement. Young English dancers, hired

Costume for the Mountain Ash Fairy in Diaghilev's *The Sleeping Princess*. Léon Bakst designed more than three hundred costumes for the 1921 production.

to fill out the large corps, were instructed by Cecchetti in the pure Russian style of Petipa and the Maryinsky. The lead roles were danced by Russian émigrés, former principals from the Imperial Theatres. And Carlotta Brianza, the first Princess Aurora, was cast as Carabosse.

As if a prophesy, the dress rehearsal was a disaster — Aurora fell during her first variation, the wrong backdrops were lowered, costumes got caught in the scenery. Despite its splendor, *The Sleeping Princess* ran for only 115 performances. The public, now accustomed to evenings of several short, exotic, and dissimilar ballets, thought the production long and old-fashioned.

Despite the financial failure, *The Sleeping Princess* (and a one-act divertissement called *Aurora's Wedding*, which Diaghilev restaged the following year for the one hundredth anniversary of Petipa's birth) was an important milestone in the history of ballet, especially in England. The original St. Petersburg production of *The Sleeping Beauty* had aroused in Benois, Bakst, and Diaghilev "an irresistible enthusiasm, a sort of delirium" for ballet, according to Benois. Likewise, Diaghilev's production inspired a love for classical ballet in a new generation of young dancers and balletomanes that resulted, in the 1930s, in the creation of Britain's first permanent ballet companies.

Bankrupt, Diaghilev was forced to leave England temporarily. He settled his company in southern France and changed its name to Les Ballets Russes de Monte Carlo. The final eight years of the company would see the production of a series of novel, inventive, and experimental ballets. Diaghilev would launch the careers of several exceptional dancers and two important choreographers — Bronislava Nijinska (1891–1972), the first woman to choreograph for the Ballets Russes, and George Balanchine (1904–1983), the great choreographic genius of the twentieth century.

*Chapter 20*

# After the War

The reaction to World War I's devastation and loss of life — ten million dead, twenty million wounded — was a post-war euphoria, a feeling that despite all the horror, humankind had survived. The 1920s were a period of social and cultural change during which all the old values, morals, and attitudes were questioned. In Russia, the survivors of the revolution and the civil war that followed were transforming what remained of the czarist empire into the Union of Soviet Socialist Republics. In the brief period before Joseph Stalin consolidated his totalitarian power and closed off Soviet society from the West, literature, painting, and even dance enjoyed an extraordinary time marked by experimentation and no government censorship. In Europe and America, writers, artists, and musicians were exploring even further than they had before the war new, sometimes shocking ways of explaining and portraying their world. It was the Jazz Age, the Roaring Twenties, a time when it seemed that anything was possible and everything permissible.

There were still no permanent national ballet companies in America or England, but dance lovers on both sides of the Atlantic were flocking to see ballerina Anna Pavlova and her traditional interpretations of classical ballet or attending the innovative recitals given by the modern dance pioneers. Novel and experimental ballets, however, were still the province of the Diaghilev company.

In 1923, for the Paris season, Diaghilev made one last attempt to present a ballet with a Russian theme, atmosphere, and music. *Les Noces (The Wedding)*, considered one of Bronislava Nijinska's two masterpieces, portrays the austere customs and rituals surrounding a peasant wedding in old Russia. The ballet includes traditional circle dances around the Bride and Groom. But much of the choreography is stylized — stark, modern, and architectural; the corps moves in monumental blocklike groups. *Les Noces* is set to a cantata by Stravinsky, scored for vocal soloists and mixed chorus (who sing fragments of Russian folk songs), four pianos, bells, xylophones, kettledrums, and other percussion instruments. The brown-and-white costumes and a set of wooden platforms by Russian artist Nathalie Gontcharova reflected the spareness and simplicity of the choreography.

Nijinska's next work (also considered one of her best) was the first of several clever, satirical, topical ballets that she did for the company during the 1920s. *Les Biches* (*The Does*, the popular slang of the day for young women) is set at a fashionable house party where the guests — young debutantes, flappers, and their athletic boyfriends — gossip and flirt. But the 1924 ballet is really a plotless suite of dances in the classical style with a little bit of acrobatics tossed in. (Athletics were much in the news that season, for Paris was hosting the Summer Olympic Games.) The music was commissioned from Francis Poulenc, an avant-garde composer in his early twenties, who provided a sophisticated score that had elements of popular jazz.

*Les Biches* was a great success and gave Diaghilev and Nijinska the idea for her next ballet that year, also a satirical look at the activities of the very people who flocked to applaud Les Ballets Russes de Monte Carlo. *Le Train Bleu* (*The Blue Train*) was named after the well-known overnight express from Paris to the Riviera resorts, the favorite vacation spot of wealthy young men and women. It depicted their beach games and seaside play — swimming, acrobatics, golf, and tennis; the dancers wore chic bathing suits created by the famous fashion designer Coco Chanel. The jolly, tuneful score was by French composer Darius Milhaud, and Picasso contributed a curtain depicting larger-than-life women frolicking on a beach.

Nijinska's ballets were popular in the 1920s. They were fashionable and stylish, a perfect representation of their time. In the 1970s and 1980s, her work was rediscovered and restaged, enabling a new generation of balletgoers to enjoy its wit and humor.

## Chapter 21

# The Immortal Pavlova

While Diaghilev was thrilling audiences with his new and exciting productions reflecting the exuberance of the Jazz Age, ballerina Anna Pavlova was bringing a more traditional form of classical ballet to the four corners of the world.

Anna Pavlova was born on January 31, 1881, in a poor district of St. Petersburg. Born two months premature, she was a tiny baby, frail and sickly, and not certain to survive. Her mother was a laundress; her father died when Anna was just two.

In 1890, for a birthday treat, Anna's mother took her to one of the first performances of *The Sleeping Beauty*. The long ride through the cold snowy streets, the brightness and warmth of the Maryinsky Theatre, and the splendors she saw on the stage changed Anna's life. During the performance, she turned to her mother and solemnly swore, "One day I shall be the Princess and shall dance on the stage of this theater."

Even at this early age, Anna had a streak of iron determination. She insisted on taking dancing lessons and then, at the age of ten, on being brought to the auditions for potential students at the Imperial Ballet School. Although she was delicate and slender, her natural grace and poetic expressiveness were already evident. So was her exotic beauty — her thick, dark hair, soulful eyes, and mysterious Mona Lisa smile. Accepted into the school, she studied with the great teachers of the day — Gerdt, Cecchetti, and Johannsen — and she was a favorite of Petipa during his last years as ballet master.

Pavlova was different, and her unique talents were immediately recognized. At a time when the robust style of the Italian ballerinas was applauded, her fragile grace echoed an older, gentler style. Like Marie Taglioni, Pavlova, who was just five feet tall, was thin and long-limbed, with liquid arms. And also like Taglioni, she was exceptionally strong and had perfect balance — she used practically no supportive blocking in her size 1½ toe shoes. On graduation Pavlova was made a soloist at the Maryinsky without first having to dance in the corps, as was the usual procedure. Within a few years, she was a prima ballerina.

Pavlova was able to transcend even the most sentimental or trite of ballets, because she had that rare ability, like Nijinsky, to become the character she was dancing — whether Giselle, a butterfly, a snowflake, or a flower. No matter how many times she danced a role, it always seemed as if she were dancing it for the first time.

For a 1905 charity concert in Russia, Fokine had improvised a short dramatic solo for Pavlova. Less than four minutes long, it would become the enduring symbol of her personality and art, a ballet she would dance thousands of times during her career. *The Dying Swan*, set to Camille Saint-Saëns's "Carnival of the Animals," is a very simple dance consisting of bourrée steps on pointe and fluttering hand and arm movements. It was Pavlova's genius that made this interpretation of the final moments of a swan into a magical and overwhelmingly emotional experience for countless audiences. Fokine called it a ballet "that penetrates the soul."

Pavlova made her first tour outside of Russia in 1908, traveling to Scandinavia with a group of Maryinsky dancers. Her fame quickly spread, and crowds of admirers often followed her back to her hotel. Pavlova recorded in her autobiography that after one such display of adoration, she asked her maid, "What have I done? Why do they love

Anna Pavlova in her most famous role, *The Dying Swan*, a short solo choreographed for her by Fokine.

me so?" The maid replied, "Madame, you have made them happy. You have let them forget for an hour the sadness of their lives." This reply set the seal on Pavlova's life. "I want to dance for the whole world," she once said. She now began to make that dream a reality.

Pavlova danced briefly with Diaghilev's Ballets Russes, during their 1909 Paris season. Being a star, however, she was never really happy about the subordinate role ballerinas played in his company. Her artistic tastes were essentially conservative and conventional, and she was not comfortable with avant-garde productions.

Inspired by Taglioni's travels, Pavlova decided to form her own touring company to bring classical ballet to the entire world. She was the art's greatest missionary and zealously sought to bring its beauty, excitement, and poetry to the four corners of the globe. In addition to touring Europe and England (her home beginning in 1912), Pavlova and her troupe visited a staggering number of countries: the United States, Canada, Mexico, Cuba, Ecuador, Costa Rica, Argentina, Peru, Japan, Malay, Singapore, Burma, Java, China, Australia, New Zealand, South Africa, India, and Egypt. Between 1910 and 1931, she traveled over five hundred thousand miles by boat and train — the equivalent of fourteen times around the equator — giving more than four thousand performances.

Pavlova made the first of her seven tours of North America in 1910. Very few classical dancers had come to the United States since Fanny Elssler's visit in 1840, and there was no homegrown ballet tradition. Pavlova's American sponsors were afraid that audiences might not understand the nature of ballet. Their ads called it "visual opera" and claimed that Pavlova was "introducing a new art to America, the interpretation of the ponderous messages of the great composers through the most primitive and yet potent of mediums — motion!" They need not have worried. America loved her. One newspaper compared her dancing to another wonder of the age: "the mid-air gyrations" of the airplane. Ballet lessons started to become popular for little girls across the country.

No stage was too big or too small for the "Sublime Pavlova." She was equally at home dancing before peasants or kings. At New York's giant Hippodrome, her troupe gave two performances a day for three months, sharing the music hall stage with acrobats, trained elephants, a chorus of West Point cadets, and a four-hundred-member minstrel show. Her contribution to this spectacle, aptly named "The Big Show," was an abbreviated version of *The Sleeping Beauty,* the first production of this classic to be seen in the United States. In Mexico City, before thirty-six thousand spectators, she performed in a bullring every Sunday afternoon for eight weeks; in Panama her theater was a warehouse on the canal, the huge doors kept open so people on

Anna Pavlova on tour.

the passing boats could see the performance. In Nashville she danced in a mission hall; the audience sat in the pews. In a small town in Cuba, she performed for an audience of one.

Pavlova never retired. In January 1931, preparing for yet another tour of Europe, she insisted on rehearsing, despite having a fever. Arriving at The Hague, in the Netherlands, a few days later, she collapsed with pneumonia. She died a week before her fiftieth birthday, whispering to her maid, "Prepare my swan costume."

To a newspaper reporter, Anna Pavlova once said, "Dancing is my gift and my life. . . . God gave me this gift to bring delight to others. That is why I was born. I am haunted by the need to dance." That burning need made it possible for hundreds of thousands of people all over the world to experience firsthand the glories of ballet and inspired a generation of boys and girls to study dance.

## Chapter 22

# Enter Balanchine

In 1924, a small group of dancers from the newly formed Soviet Union joined the Diaghilev company. Among them was a talented dancer and budding choreographer from the former Imperial Theatre Ballet School, a twenty-year-old named Georgi Melitonovitch Balanchivadze. Within a few months, his dancing career cut short by injury, he had become the company's chief choreographer and had changed his name to George Balanchine.

Despite his youth, Balanchine had already created ballets in Russia, the first in 1920. These had been influenced by experimental works being done in his homeland by avant-garde dancers and choreographers who were introducing both athleticism and eroticism into ballet. Diaghilev gave Balanchine his first opportunity to work with the foremost composers and artists in the West — including Stravinsky, Satie, Matisse, Utrillo, Miró, and Derain.

In 1928, Balanchine choreographed his first original work to Stravinsky's music, the beginning of a collaboration that would last more than forty years. *Apollon Musagète*, or *Apollo, Leader of the Muses*, is considered the first ballet done in the neoclassical, or contemporary classical, style that would be Balanchine's hallmark. *Apollo*, as the ballet is now known, is a suite of dances for the young Greek and Roman god of music and poetry and the Muses who receive their gifts of art from him.

Serge Lifar as Apollo and Alexandra Danilova as the Muse of
Dance, Terpsichore, in the "swimming" movement in the original
production of George Balanchine's *Apollon Musagète* (1928).
Danilova, who had left the Soviet Union with George Balanchine
in 1924, eventually came to America, where for many years she
was the country's favorite ballerina and then a noted teacher.

Balanchine said that this ballet was the turning point of his life.
Taking his lead from Stravinsky's stripped down yet melodic score
for a string orchestra, the choreographer simplified the vocabulary of
classical ballet but did not diminish its clarity and precision. "In its
discipline and restraint . . . the score was a revelation. It seemed to
tell me that I could dare *not* use everything, that I, too, could elimi-
nate." Balanchine was interested in using old steps in new ways to
extend the potential and limits of what the human body could do in
space. He enlarged the vocabulary of the classical ballet language.
He discarded the fussy conventions of academic ballet but kept the

90-degree turnout, the five basic positions, and all the steps, jumps, and beats of the *ballet d'école*. To these he added steps and movements that were more modern and up-to-date. He had the dancers turn in their feet, jut out their hips, bend their knees when turning, contract their torsos. Feet could be pointed, but they could also be flexed. Arms might be held in a correct port de bras or the wrists and elbows held at strange angles. Movements might be serene or graceful, or they could be gymnastic or distorted. A ballerina might be supported in off-balance turns or held in unusual positions.

The roots of Balanchine's new style were firmly planted in the Petipa heritage, which included intricate combinations of steps and a love for geometric patterns. But unlike Petipa, Balanchine didn't have preconceived ideas about what a ballet would look like. He let it evolve as he worked with the dancers.

Balanchine also had a finely cultivated appreciation of music and its importance to dance. The son of a well-known Georgian composer, Balanchine had studied piano at the same conservatory as had Tchaikovsky. Balanchine felt that musical tempos should never be slowed down or speeded up to fit the choreography or a dancer's preference. A score should be played as indicated by the composer. In his ballets, Balanchine, who claimed "the music dictates the whole shape of the work," tried to make the music visible, wanting his choreography to clearly express its meaning. He wanted audiences to "see the music, hear the dance."

George Balanchine was the choreographer of *Prodigal Son*, the last ballet commissioned and presented by Diaghilev. This collaboration with composer Sergei Prokofiev and religious artist Georges Rouault, who created scenery that looked like stained-glass windows, was strikingly different from the frivolous ballets of the period. *Prodigal Son* was an emotional, expressionistic, and dramatic retelling of a biblical parable. It tells the story of a defiant young man who, longing for excitement, leaves home, encounters evil and sin, then

COSTAS

Mikhail Baryshnikov in the title role of Balanchine's *Prodigal Son*. The ballet, choreographed in 1929 for the Ballets Russes, is still in the active repertoire and uses the original costume and scenic designs of Georges Rouault.

returns, contrite, to the accepting arms of his father. The ballet premiered on May 21, 1929.

Within three months of that premiere, Serge Diaghilev was dead, the fortune-teller's prophecy having come true — he died on water, in Venice, the city of canals. Diaghilev, the man who had "splashed Paris with color," had influenced European culture for twenty years, changing the way people thought about ballet and music. The Ballets Russes had presented sixty-three ballets, and Diaghilev had encouraged the careers of important dancers, choreographers, composers, designers, and artists. Left leaderless without him, the Ballets Russes disbanded.

*Chapter 23* 🙢

# The 1930s

In October 1929, the crash of the New York stock market, followed by a chain reaction of similar crashes in Europe, brought an abrupt end to the post-war prosperity and euphoria. A long period of worldwide economic collapse and hardship, known as the Great Depression, followed. Fascism and militant nationalism were on the rise all across Europe, bringing with them all kinds of persecution and oppression — political, cultural, and religious. The creative centers of ballet were shifting. More and more artists, writers, composers, choreographers, and dancers were fleeing to England or emigrating to the safety of the United States. Ballet's history began to take on a different accent — not French or Russian, but English.

By the end of the decade, only twenty-one years after World War I, the world was once again plunged into global conflict. World War II (1939–1945) pitted the Allies (the United States, Great Britain, France, and the Soviet Union) against the totalitarian Axis powers (Germany, Italy, and Japan). By 1941, the Nazis had occupied most of Europe. They considered most contemporary art to be "degenerate." The Nazis burned books, banned performances, put critics of their regime into concentration camps, and even murdered them. But according to Edward Denby, the most important dance writer of the day, "Wartime [in America and England] made everyone more eager for the civilized and peaceful excitement of ballet."

However, the 1930s did not begin auspiciously for lovers of ballet. The Ballets Russes had been dissolved in 1929. Anna Pavlova's death eighteen months later left the ballet world without the companies that had carried the art throughout Europe and America. But more than ever before, audiences needed entertainments that could transport them away from the harsh realities of their everyday lives. Although Europe's permanent ballet companies — those associated with the great opera houses — continued to give performances during the 1930s, they were, for the most part, tired institutions presenting the same kinds of ballets that had been performed for decades. Although the economic times were bad, it was not long before an attempt was made to recapture the glamour and box office magic of Diaghilev's old company.

In 1932, René Blum, the manager of the Monte Carlo Theater, and Colonel Wassily de Basil, an ex–Cossack officer and businessman with a passion for ballet, reunited many of the stars of the original Ballets Russes in an effort to preserve the Diaghilev repertoire, costumes, and scenery. The group included Nijinska, Fokine, Massine, and for a short while, Balanchine. This company, Ballet Russe de Monte Carlo, and later spin-off groups, toured constantly. Over the next twenty years, they built an audience for ballets both classical and experimental in the United States, Europe, and Australia. The Ballet Russe de Monte Carlo also introduced a new generation of ballet fans to great dancers such as Frederic Franklin, André Eglevsky, and Alexandra Danilova. By the mid–1940s, many of the dancers in this "Russian" company were American.

Léonide Massine had become the chief choreographer of the Blum/de Basil company in the early 1930s. For the original Ballets Russes, he had created lighthearted works that combined mime and classical technique. He now turned to more serious plotless dances, creating three great symphonic ballets, choreographic interpretations of well-known concert hall scores, music previously thought undanceable: *Les Présages* (1933), to Tchaikovsky's Fifth Symphony; *Choreartium* (1933), to Brahm's Fourth Symphony; and *Symphonie Fantastique* (1936), to Berlioz's Third Symphony. At the time, these ballets were considered avant-garde, but they opened up a whole range of musical possibilities for future choreographers.

While the new incarnations of the Ballets Russes (under several different names and managers) were trying to carry on Diaghilev's traditions, another former dancer with the company, the impresario's last protégé and great male dancer, was bringing French ballet into the twentieth century. Serge Lifar (1905–1986), a startlingly handsome young man from Kiev, had danced the title roles in *Apollo* and *Prodigal Son*. Within two weeks of Diaghilev's death, Lifar, twenty-four, was invited to join the Paris Opera as principal dancer and choreographer. He soon was made artistic director and immediately began to reorganize and modernize the company's repertoire, which was stuck in the nineteenth century.

Meanwhile, in the United States during the 1930s, a native tradition of classical dance was evolving. America's first regional ballet company, the San Francisco Ballet, was founded in 1933. A year later, American dancer and choreographer Ruth Page (born in 1905 in Indianapolis) was appointed ballet director of the Chicago Grand Opera Company; within a few years she formed the Chicago Opera Ballet. In 1935, the short-lived Philadelphia Ballet was founded by dancer, choreographer, and teacher Catherine Littlefield (1904–1951). This was the country's first ballet company with an American-born director. During the 1930s, George Balanchine, who had arrived in New York in 1933, was beginning the long process of creating works using a new American vocabulary, choreographed in America specifically for American dancers and audiences.

## Chapter 24 ～
# Ballet in England

At the same time that ballet was being revitalized in France and the United States in the years leading up to the Second World War, the seeds of Britain's first national ballet were being planted.

The British have long been lovers of dance. It was a favorite pastime of kings, queens, and courtiers in the fifteenth and sixteenth centuries. By the time the monarchy was restored in 1660, ballet and dance had become public, rather than royal, entertainments. Soon the first in a long line of foreign dancers arrived in England to perform. Sallé, Taglioni, Grisi, Grahn, Cerrito, Perrot, Pavlova, Karsavina, and Nijinsky were all popular with London audiences. Dance entertainments had been featured in music halls and theaters since the late 1800s. London also became the home of several fine ballet schools — both Enrico Cecchetti and Tamara Karsavina began teaching there in 1918. So it was surprising that unlike other European capitals, London, in the third decade of the twentieth century, still did not have its own permanent ballet company.

The establishment of serious, national ballet companies in Great Britain came about through the hard work of two women, neither of whom was English by birth.

Dame Marie Rambert (1888–1982), born in Warsaw, Poland, had come to London to study with Isadora Duncan and Emile Jaques-Dalcroze. When she was hired by Diaghilev in 1913 to help teach Nijinsky's complicated counts in *The Rite of Spring* to the Ballets

Russes' dancers, she also had the opportunity to study classical ballet technique with Cecchetti. Rambert, like Diaghilev, had a gift for discovering and nurturing the talent of others. She opened her own London school in 1920, and ten years later, she and her husband founded the Ballet Club. By 1933, they were staging regular Sunday evening performances. The couple had purchased and converted a tiny church hall with only one hundred seats, naming it the Mercury Theatre. This obscure theater, far away from London's West End theater district, was the place to see famous guest artists — Alicia Markova, Tamara Karsavina, and such budding talents as the young American dancer-choreographer Agnes de Mille.

The Mercury was also the seedbed for England's future choreographers. Rambert was the first to encourage the two men who are considered the great British choreographers of the twentieth century: Frederick Ashton (1904–1988), whose ballets would come to define the British style of ballet, and Antony Tudor (1908–1987), the pioneer of the psychological ballet-drama.

Antony Tudor joined the dance world relatively late in life. He was a clerk in a London market when he fell in love with ballet at the age of nineteen after seeing Pavlova and the Ballets Russes. He started taking lessons with Marie Rambert, then joined the Mercury Theatre as her secretary and stage manager. Rambert encouraged him to choreograph, and over the next five years, he created several short ballets for her company. In 1936, the Ballet Rambert, as it was now called, presented Tudor's first masterpiece, *Lilac Garden (Jardin aux Lilas)*, followed a year later by his second important work, *Dark Elegies.*

Building on Fokine's ideas about expressive dance, Tudor was also influenced by the psychoanalytic theories of Sigmund Freud. He created narrative, psychological ballets in which there are no set pieces of mime. Instead there is a continuous flow of dramatic movements based on classical technique and everyday gestures that reveal the innermost private thoughts, feelings, desires, and motivations of the characters. For example, a series of fast pirouettes might be used to indicate frenzy or anger; bounding leaps across the stage represent passion; a brief shake of the head might mean indecision. Tudor's vocabulary of gestures and body language conveyed meanings as clearly as the spoken word. He was also interested in exploring how human relationships break down under the stress of rigid social codes and conventions and in examining the mental and emotional lives of ordinary people. His ballets often deal with people in trouble.

*Lilac Garden* is a Victorian tragedy about a marriage of convenience. As the original program synopsis describes it:

> *Caroline, on the eve of her marriage to a man she does not love, tries to say farewell to her lover at a garden reception, but is constantly interrupted by guests and in the end goes off on the arm of her betrothed with hopelessness in her eyes. The situation is complicated by the presence of her betrothed's former lover.*

*Dark Elegies*, set to Gustav Mahler's *Kindertotenlieder (Songs of Childhood Death)*, is also a tragic ballet, the ritual mourning of a community sharing sorrow after the loss of their children from some unnamed disaster. The parents' sadness and pain is evoked entirely through dance movement, not mime.

Tudor left England in the late 1930s to work in the United States with Ballet Theatre (later called American Ballet Theatre). Although his output was relatively small — less than twenty ballets — Tudor's most important works remain in the active repertoire of American Ballet Theatre and other major companies.

In the 1930s and 1940s, the Ballet Rambert continued to present exciting experimental works. In the 1960s, the company was reorganized into a modern dance troupe, the Rambert Dance Company. Today it is the oldest English dance company still performing.

The other founder of British ballet is Dame Ninette de Valois, born Edris Stannus in 1896 in County Wicklow, Ireland. Like Marie Rambert, she studied with Cecchetti. Having danced professionally in the theater since she was fourteen, she joined the Diaghilev company in 1923. De Valois dreamed of founding and directing a British repertory ballet company. She wanted to present English dancers in the nineteenth-century classics but more important, to cultivate a national style, spirit, and identity. She wanted a truly English ballet that would appeal to all levels of British society, one that would use English choreographers, English composers, and English drama, novels, and poems for its source material.

De Valois left the Ballets Russes after two years to pursue her dream. She opened a school and in 1926, approached Lilian Baylis, director of London's Old Vic Theatre, with an idea. For twenty years, Baylis had made Britain's national theater the home to the best in classical English opera and Shakespearean drama. Would she allow de Valois to teach the actors movement and also have her dancers gain the experience they needed by appearing in those productions? The answer was yes, and de Valois became the ballet mistress at the Old Vic.

In 1931, when Baylis reopened the derelict Sadler's Wells Theatre (which had been built on the site of a seventeenth-century mineral spring and pleasure garden), de Valois moved her school there; her group became known as the Vic-Wells Ballet and later, the Sadler's Wells Ballet. The company — numbering at first only six dancers — presented their first full evening of ballet later that year. De Valois was their director and ballerina as well as choreographer. Three of de Valois's most important ballets, all to music by English composers, are *Job* (1935), based on biblical illustrations by nineteenth-century British artist William Blake; *The Rake's Progress* (1935), modeled on a series of famous prints by William Hogarth that trace a wealthy young man's descent into ruin in eighteenth-century

London; and *Checkmate* (1937), an allegorical chess game between Love and Death.

When former Diaghilev dancer Alicia Markova and her partner, danseur Anton Dolin, joined the company, de Valois was able, with the help of the former Maryinsky régisseur, Nicholas Sergeyev, to stage *Giselle, Swan Lake, The Nutcracker,* and *Coppélia,* the great nineteenth-century works that would be one cornerstone of her repertoire. In 1939 came an evening-length version of Petipa's *The Sleeping Beauty.* It was staged by Sergeyev and Rambert's protégé, Frederick Ashton, and its Aurora was an unknown nineteen-year-old named Margot Fonteyn (1919–1991). Fonteyn would become Ashton's muse and one of the most beloved ballerinas of the twentieth century.

De Valois continued to build the British character of the company. In 1935, she had asked Ashton to stage his sparkling and technically difficult divertissement, *Les Rendezvous,* and two years later he joined the company permanently as principal choreographer. His choreographic genius shaped British ballet for the next forty years.

Frederick Ashton, who was born in Guayaquil, Ecuador, claimed his life was changed forever when he was eleven and saw Pavlova dance. According to Ashton, Pavlova "injected the poison" of ballet into his veins. When he was sent to school in England, he had the opportunity to study with Léonide Massine, who in turn introduced his young student to Marie Rambert.

Over his long career, Ashton created a wide variety of ballets. He has been called a poet of classical dance. All of his works are imbued with what is now called the British style — a way of dancing that reflects that country's appreciation for good taste, good manners, and decorous understatement. He was a master of Petipa's classical vocabulary, and although his works are technically difficult, they appear effortless. Ashton's style is one of restrained lyricism, poetic grace, uncluttered simplicity, and refined elegance. Ashton always paid close attention to the smallest detail in the placement of the arms and body. He was also noted for his use of the pas de deux as a warm, tender duet of love, filling it with rapturous lifts and romantic partnering.

Ashton's most well known works include *Les Patineurs (The Skaters)* (1937), a merry Victorian nosegay set to themes from several Meyerbeer operas; the dancers use gliding and skimming steps, spins, and figures derived from ice-skating in a series of dances that range from dreamingly romantic to technically daring. *Symphonic Variations* (1946), to César Franck's Symphonic Variations for Piano and Orchestra, is a plotless neoclassical ballet of serene beauty. In 1948, Ashton created a three-act *Cinderella* to music by Prokofiev, the first evening-length ballet by a British choreographer. He has also done ballets adapted from Shakespeare's plays, including *Romeo and Juliet* (1955), to music by Prokofiev, and *The Dream* (1964), to music by Felix Mendelssohn, a one-act version of *A Midsummer Night's Dream*. One of his most popular ballets is an adaptation of the late eighteenth-century comic classic *La Fille Mal Gardée* (1960), in which Ashton included British folk dancing, in the form of a maypole ribbon dance, and broad humor in the style of English music halls: a clog dance done in travesty and a barnyard pas de cinq for a rooster and four hens.

During World War II, many of England's large theaters and opera houses were shut down; some, like the home of the Sadler's Wells Ballet, were destroyed during German air raids. Despite the fact that many of their male dancers were off fighting, the company continued to perform whenever possible, sometimes with bombs falling nearby.

In 1946, the Sadler's Wells Ballet was given the honor of presenting the first postwar performance at the Royal Opera House, Covent Garden, which had been closed for the duration of the war. They chose to do *The Sleeping Beauty,* in a magnificent production that starred Margot Fonteyn and her longtime partner, Australian danseur Robert Helpmann. The Sadler's Wells Ballet became the opera house's first resident ballet company, and five years later, Queen Elizabeth II granted them a charter of incorporation, creating the Royal Ballet.

Ninette de Valois retired as company director in 1963 and was succeeded by the now knighted Sir Frederick Ashton. In 1970, he was followed by Sir Kenneth MacMillan (1929–1992), a British choreographer who had studied at de Valois's Sadler's Wells School and was noted for his multi-act dramatic ballets based on literary or historical themes and sources *(Romeo and Juliet, Manon, Mayerling, Isadora, Anastasia).* Since 1986, the Royal Ballet has been under the direction of Anthony Dowell (born in 1943), formerly one of the company's most renowned classical dancers. Today the company is composed of two troupes: the London-based Royal Ballet and the Birmingham Royal Ballet.

## Chapter 25

# England's Radiant Princess and Russia's Leaping Lion

Dame Margot Fonteyn, one of the twentieth century's outstanding prima ballerinas, was born Margaret Hookham in Surrey, England, in 1919. She was four years old when she took her first dancing lesson because her parents thought it would teach her deportment. Her father's work as an engineer caused the family to move frequently. When Margot was eleven, they were living in Shanghai, where she had the chance to study with a former Maryinsky teacher who recognized her emerging talents. The young dancer and her mother returned to England so she could continue her studies at Ninette de Valois's Vic-Wells School. Fonteyn made her stage debut at fifteen, and when Alicia Markova left the Sadler's Wells Ballet to form her own company, Fonteyn, just seventeen, was chosen to perform in the great star's place.

Slender, delicate, petite, with radiant dark eyes and porcelain skin, Margot Fonteyn cast a spell of enchantment from the moment she stepped onstage. Her lyrical elegance and effortless artistry were the perfect match for Frederick Ashton's choreography of classical purity and tender delicacy. From 1935 to 1963, he created many major works for her. Her most memorable role, the one that made her internationally famous, was Princess Aurora, in *The Sleeping Beauty*. Fonteyn danced the role at her debut in the United States in

Margot Fonteyn and Rudolf Nureyev execute a perfect fish dive in Frederick Ashton's production of *The Sleeping Beauty* for the Royal Ballet.

1949, at age thirty. Her incandescent portrayal, full of youthful charm and exuberance, stunned an American audience unfamiliar with the full version of the classic. Whatever her chronological age, Fonteyn was always able to transform herself into a sixteen-year-old discovering love for the first time.

In 1961, Margot Fonteyn, then forty-two, was thinking of retiring when a political event — the daring defection from the Soviet Union of dancer Rudolf Nureyev — changed her life and the history of ballet. Nureyev (1938–1993) was an electrifying, magnetic, twenty-three-year-old virtuoso from the Kirov Ballet. Because he was the first Soviet dancer to seek political asylum in the West, his leap to freedom at Paris's Le Bourget airport made headlines around the world. Nureyev said he wanted to experience the artistic freedom he could not find in his homeland because of the restrictions imposed by Communism. His dancing in the West ushered in a new age of the male ballet superstar.

A year after his defection, Nureyev and Fonteyn danced together for the first time, appearing in a production of *Giselle* at Covent Garden. This was the beginning of a legendary partnership. For the next seventeen years, they dazzled audiences all over the world, who in return, showered them with love and adoration — on tour in Vienna, they received a record eighty-nine curtain calls for their performance in *Swan Lake*, and their memorable 1975 London debut in a new production of *Romeo and Juliet* provoked a forty-minute ovation.

Margot Fonteyn stopped dancing at the age of sixty. In 1986, she appeared on stage for the last time in the ballet most closely associated with her career, *The Sleeping Beauty*, playing the nondancing role of the Queen Mother. In 1991, Dame Margot died in Panama, where she and her husband, a Panamanian diplomat, had lived on their cattle ranch for many years.

Rudolf Nureyev's beginnings were as dramatic as his personality — he was born on a train rolling through Siberia. Although he knew he wanted to be a dancer from the time he was six years old, he did not start his ballet training until he was seventeen (a very late age for a classical danseur). Since his family was poor, there had been no money for lessons, and his father, a soldier, did not consider ballet a suitable career for his son. When Nureyev finally entered the Kirov School, his talent was immediately recognized. He was athletic, exotic, and theatrical, a dancer whose raw vigor and smoldering passion always commanded center stage. Nureyev became the most widely known dancer in history. He toured constantly, dancing with ballet and modern dance companies. He performed on all the world's great stages, in films, and on television. He was also a choreographer and a conductor, and for several years was director of the Paris Opera Ballet. His magnetic charisma made him a media star, and he attracted millions of new fans to ballet. He brought a new sense of magic and excitement to classical ballets as well as to contemporary works from the modern dance repertoire. His dramatic ability was as legendary as his technical prowess. Fonteyn, who compared him to "a young lion leaping," said "his breathtaking steps sometimes [looked] as easy as a bird flying, sometimes dangerously impossible."

Nureyev never publicly announced his retirement. "The main thing," he said in a 1990 interview, "is dancing, and before it withers away from my body, I will keep dancing till the last moment, the last drop." The greatest male dancer since Nijinsky died of complications from AIDS in Paris in 1993.

## Chapter 26

# Ballet in America: A Star-Spangled Start

The story of how permanent ballet companies finally became established in the United States begins in the 1920s and 1930s, when European and Russian dancers and choreographers started to arrive in ever greater numbers. They were not the first foreign dancers to cross the Atlantic to teach or entertain Americans. French and English dancing masters had visited America during colonial times to instruct rich landowners of the Carolinas and Virginia (including George Washington) in the minuet and the gavotte. A British dancer named Henry Holt gave theatrical performances in Charleston in 1735, and pantomimes and "ballet-spectacles" were presented in theaters in New York, Philadelphia, and Baltimore before the Revolutionary War. Americans liked to dance. During pioneer days, ordinary people enjoyed participating in spirited barn dances, square dances, and Virginia reels, and ballroom dances such as the waltz were popular throughout the nineteenth century.

Despite their distance from the ballet centers of Europe, Americans did have some opportunities to experience classical dance. French dancers started to visit the United States in the early 1820s; *La Sylphide* was performed in 1835, *Giselle* eleven years later. The Petipa family danced in New York City in 1839, Fanny Elssler toured the country in the early 1840s, and Carlotta Brianza came in 1883.

Augusta Maywood, America's first internationally known ballerina, in her debut at the age of twelve in 1837.

Although most of the classical dancers seen by Americans during the nineteenth century were European in origin, the United States could boast of two native-born ballerinas: Mary Ann Lee (1823–1899) and Augusta Maywood (1825–1876), as well as one native-born danseur: George Washington Smith (1820–1899). Lee's parents were circus performers — her mother a dancer, her father an acrobat. She was born and trained in Philadelphia and as a girl sang and danced in a P. T. Barnum troupe to help support her family after her parents' deaths. She was the first ballerina to dance *Giselle* in the United States, after going to Paris to study with Jules Perrot and Jean Coralli. Lee's partner, George Washington Smith, was the first American to dance the role of Albrecht.

Augusta Maywood's name spread far beyond the borders of the United States. She was the first American dancer to gain international fame, and for one hundred years was the only American recognized as a ballerina. At twelve, Maywood, who came from a family of actors, was already a professional dancer. She and Lee debuted in the same ballet, an adaptation of Filippo Taglioni's *Le Dieu et la Bayadère*. At fifteen she became the first American to be admitted to the Royal Academy and dance at the Paris Opera. Maywood received star billing for her portrayal of Giselle throughout Europe and was praised for her strength and speed. She eventually settled in Italy, had five children, and formed her own touring troupe, the first traveling ballet company. Until she retired in 1862, Maywood performed in the great Romantic classics and in her own ballet version of Harriet Beecher Stowe's *Uncle Tom's Cabin*.

America, at the end of the nineteenth century, still did not have any homegrown classical dance companies. Theatrical dancing, associated with music halls, beer gardens, and vaudeville, was considered something not quite moral. This disdain had its roots in the country's Puritan past. And ballet, an art form created by and for royalty, carried with it an aristocratic taint, which many felt made it inappropriate for a democratic society such as the United States. But during the early years of the new century, visits by the great European troupes and dancers helped change public opinion about ballet.

Pavlova's cross-country tours, beginning in 1910, instituted a vogue for ballet in the United States. To satisfy the artistic longings of young girls and their mothers and to supply the corps de ballet needed by visiting ballerinas, dance schools sprang up all over America. Many were run by European dancers and choreographers who began to make the United States their home during the 1920s. Early in the decade, Michel Fokine settled in New York City, and Adolph Bolm, a Russian-born former Ballets Russes dancer, opened a school in San Francisco. In 1933, the San Francisco Opera established a ballet company under Bolm's direction; the San Francisco Ballet (and its school) is the oldest continuous professional ballet company in the United States.

In 1924, Mikhail Mordkin, a former Bolshoi dancer and Pavlova's partner on her early American tours, decided to remain in New York City and open a school. Among his pupils were a young Judy Garland and Vaslav and Romola Nijinsky's daughter, Kyra. In 1937, he formed the Mordkin Ballet. Two years later, the company of ninety-one, known as Ballet Theatre (later called American Ballet Theatre, or ABT), announced its artistic policy: to present "the best that is traditional, the best that is contemporary, and inevitably, the best that is controversial," in a repertoire that would include works from many different times and by many different choreographers, including Americans. From its beginning, Ballet Theatre was a national touring company that relied on American and European stars. Fokine, Massine, Nijinska, and Dolin restaged ballets for the company, and Antony Tudor was the company's resident choreographer for many years. His *Pillar of Fire* (1942) was responsible for the emergence of America's first great dramatic ballerina, New York–born Nora Kaye. She received twenty curtain calls for her electrifying debut as Hagar, the insecure woman who commits a shameful indiscretion because she believes the man she loves prefers her pretty young sister.

Over the years, many international stars have danced with ABT, including

| from Cuba: | Alicia Alonso (founder of the National Ballet of Cuba) |
| from Denmark: | Erik Bruhn |
| from Germany: | Richard Cragun (born in the United States) and Marcia Haydée (born in Brazil, now director of the Stuttgart Ballet) |

from Great Britain:      Anthony Dowell, Margot Fonteyn, and
                         Lynn Seymour (born in Canada)
from Hungary:            Ivan Nagy
from Italy:              Carla Fracci
from the Soviet Union:   Mikhail Baryshnikov, Natalia Makarova,
                         and Rudolf Nureyev
from the United States:  Fernando Bujones, Melissa Hayden
                         (born in Canada), Gelsey Kirkland,
                         Maria Tallchief (the first Native
                         American prima ballerina), Violette
                         Verdy (born in France), and Sallie
                         Wilson

While ABT and the San Francisco Ballet were attempting to establish permanent classical ballet companies in the United States, two men — a brilliant Russian-born choreographer who had worked with Diaghilev and an equally brilliant American, the heir to a Boston department store fortune — were developing a truly American ballet.

## *A Number of Firsts: The San Francisco Ballet*

The San Francisco Ballet, founded in 1933, is the oldest continuous professional company in the United States. From the 1940s through the 1960s, the company was shaped by three brothers, the descendants of Danish dance and music teachers who had settled in Utah in 1854. Willam, Harold, and Lew Christensen were dancers, choreographers, and teachers; Lew was considered America's first male classical dancer.

The San Francisco Ballet was the first American company to produce a full-length *Sleeping Beauty* (1940), and they presented the first *Nutcracker* ever performed in its entirety in the Western Hemisphere

(1944). In 1980, their codirector, choreographer Michael Smuin, created *The Tempest* (based on Shakespeare's play), the first full-length ballet to have original music, designs, and choreography created by American-born artists. Since 1985, the company has been directed by Helgi Tomasson, a former New York City Ballet principal dancer who was born in Reykjavík, Iceland, in 1942. The San Francisco Ballet is known for its polish, precision, and verve and a dancing style that combines the grandness of traditional classicism with the freshness of today. For his company, Tomasson has choreographed a number of neoclassical ballets noted for their lyricism, elegance, and musicality, the same qualities he showed as a dancer.

## Chapter 27
# "But First a School"

The man responsible in great part for laying the foundations for a classical ballet tradition in the United States was, like Diaghilev, neither a choreographer nor a dancer. But like the great Ballets Russes impresario, he was someone with a dream — to create a truly American ballet every bit as good as the ones in Europe.

Lincoln Kirstein was born in Rochester, New York, in 1907 but as a young child moved to Boston, where his father was co-owner of Filene's department store. From an early age, Kirstein was attracted to the arts. As a Harvard undergraduate, he helped found and edit an influential literary quarterly and established the Harvard Society for Contemporary Art. The Society mounted the first Boston exhibitions of artists who were changing the face of twentieth-century art — Picasso, Matisse, Alexander Calder, Edward Hopper, Georgia O'Keeffe, R. Buckminster Fuller, and others.

Kirstein's love affair with ballet began when he was a teenager. His parents had refused to let him see the Ballets Russes during their 1916 American tour because they thought their ballets were not appropriate for a nine-year-old, although they took him to see Pavlova three years later. During a summer spent in London when he was fifteen, Kirstein was finally allowed to see Diaghilev's company, and he went to performances every night. Then, in August of 1929, when Kirstein was twenty-two, something happened that the young man later saw as prophetic. After spending his junior year studying art in Italy, he was sightseeing in Venice. Stepping inside an old church on an out-of-the-way street, he came upon a group of mourners. Attracted by the beauty of the Orthodox service, he stayed. Two days later, he found out that the funeral he had witnessed had been Diaghilev's.

After Kirstein graduated from college, his intense and idealistic passion to create an American ballet tradition continued to grow. Kirstein knew that there was only one choreographer innovative enough to help him accomplish his dream: George Balanchine. In 1933, he approached the gifted but then out-of-work choreographer in Paris and presented him with a proposition: Would he come to the United States to head a company of American dancers dancing American ballets? The initial backing for this venture would come from Kirstein's father and the wealthy family of a Harvard school-friend, Edward M. M. Warburg. The young Russian, who loved American jazz and the dancing of Hollywood film stars Fred Astaire and Ginger Rogers, agreed, with one condition: "But first a school," he said. Before he could build a company, he needed a place where he could train dancers in a new style. He envisioned an approach based on the pure classical traditions of Petipa and the Maryinsky yet adapted to and expressive of the American physique and the American way of moving. Balanchine later called his adopted country "the land of lovely bodies." He admired the freedom with which Americans moved, their long-limbed athleticism and speed, and his new school and company would incorporate and express this dynamic energy.

The School of American Ballet (SAB) opened on New Year's Day, 1934, in New York City, in a shabby, one-room studio once owned by Isadora Duncan. The next day, twenty-five pupils began classes. Balanchine immediately set to work to show that American dancers could look as noble and as beautiful as those trained in Europe or Russia.

His first ballet created in America with American dancers was *Serenade* (1934), to Tchaikovsky's lush Serenade in C for Strings. Although it was a ballet made specifically for students, with the focus on the ensemble, it is considered a masterpiece and today, like many of Balanchine's ballets, is performed by companies around the world.

*Serenade* originated as a lesson in stage technique for his students, a way to teach them the differences between dancing in a classroom and dancing on stage as part of a large group, something

The opening tableau in *Serenade*, the first ballet created by George Balanchine in America (1934). It is now the signature work of the New York City Ballet, the company founded by Balanchine and Lincoln Kirstein.

most of them had never done, despite their technical skills. Balanchine choreographed the sections of the ballet on the students he had available at the time. The first evening there were seventeen girls, so this is the number in the first section. The next night there were only nine girls, then only six. During one rehearsal a dancer tripped and fell, and that movement was left in the ballet. Another time, one arrived late and had trouble finding her place, and that, too, was included in the choreography, as a delayed entrance. When boys began attending class, choreography for them was added.

Despite the seemingly haphazard and piecemeal way in which it was created, *Serenade* was and still is a masterpiece of pure dancing. Combining an atmosphere of Romantic nineteenth-century ballet with the contemporary, athletic technique of the twentieth, its movements are softer and rounder than those in Balanchine's later, more sharp-edged ballets. *Serenade*, which contains many beautiful patterns and designs, has no narrative or plot, although it and the music are filled with emotion and feeling. Balanchine said it is "simply, dancers in motion to a beautiful piece of music. The only story is the music's story . . . a dance in the light of the moon."

A few months after *Serenade* was first performed — for invited guests at the Warburg family's Westchester estate — Balanchine, Kirstein, and Warburg decided that their students were ready for public performances. They named the troupe the American Ballet. The early years of the fledgling company were difficult — short seasons were followed by long periods of inactivity. The middle of the Great Depression wasn't a very good time to start a ballet company. There were not many well-trained American dancers, and the audience for classical dance was small. In 1938, Kirstein told a magazine reporter, "Transplanting ballet to this country is like trying to raise a palm tree in Dakota." Ballet was still considered a European rather than American art form.

For three years, the American Ballet was the resident company of the Metropolitan Opera in New York, but Balanchine's choreographic ideas — too experimental and too sexy, said some — upset not only the Opera's director and the singers but the staid and conservative opera audience. There were constant arguments between Balanchine and the management. Broadway and Hollywood, however, appreciated Balanchine's inventive theatrical skills: he choreographed the first of nineteen stage musicals, *On Your Toes*, in 1936 and the first of four movies, *Goldwyn Follies*, two years later. *On Your Toes* was the first Broadway musical to use ballet. The plot revolves around the onstage and backstage life of a Russian ballet company on tour in the United States, rehearsing and premiering a ballet called *Slaughter on Tenth Avenue*. Unlike previous dance numbers on Broadway, *Slaughter* was an actual part of the story line, instead of an interruption in the action of the play.

When American Ballet's contract with the Metropolitan Opera was not renewed in 1938, Balanchine became a freelance choreographer. Over the next six years, he continued to work in film and musicals while remounting or creating new pieces for the Ballet Russe de Monte Carlo, the Paris Opera, and American Ballet Theatre.

In 1941, Kirstein, with the backing of the U.S. State Department, organized American Ballet Caravan for a six-month goodwill tour of South America. For this trip, Balanchine created two of his most important and enduring works: *Ballet Imperial* (now, like many of his ballets, simply called after the music, *Tchaikovsky Concerto #2*) and *Concerto Barocco*, to Bach's Concerto in D Minor for Two Violins.

As its original name implied, *Ballet Imperial* was an homage to the grandeur, opulence, and classical purity of Petipa and the Maryinsky. Its steps and movements are courtly, graceful, and precise, the dances for the ensemble have passion, and the variations are brilliant and technically difficult. *Concerto Barocco* is filled with formal patterns of geometric symmetry that mirror the pristine yet often lively Baroque music. The ballet is by turns elegant and jaunty and contains many interweaving images. The corps of eight women is always on stage and is as prominent as the two ballerinas. In a

Balanchine ballet, the corps often does movements that are the same as or equally difficult as those done by the soloists.

Both *Ballet Imperial* and *Concerto Barocco* originally had elaborate costumes and scenery — Balanchine once compared the large, stiff tutus in *Ballet Imperial* to "giant mudpies." Today, both dances, like many Balanchine ballets, are performed without decor and in simpler costumes. In 1948, when the choreographer finally got his own company, the New York City Ballet, there was very little money for extras such as backdrops, sets, costumes. So, many of the ballets were performed on a bare stage, the dancers in stark practice clothes — black-and-white leotards or tunics for the women, black tights and white T-shirts for the men. This early necessity, which focuses the eye on the choreography and allows the dancers' bodies to be clearly seen, eventually became one of the trademarks of Balanchine's company and style.

American Ballet Caravan also presented ballets with purely American themes. One was based on the opening of the American frontier and the legend of the notorious desperado William Bonney, better known as Billy the Kid, who terrorized the Southwest in the late 1870s. *Billy the Kid* (1938), choreographed by Milwaukee-born Eugene Loring (1914–1982), was the first ballet to tell a story out of the country's pioneering past. The ballet had a libretto by Lincoln Kirstein and a score by Brooklyn-born composer Aaron Copland. Loring, who had studied with Fokine and Massine, used classical steps and technique but also relied on stylized gestures of fighting, roping, riding, shooting, and card playing to characterize the people, setting, and period.

In 1946, with the Depression and World War II behind them, Balanchine and Kirstein established a new company, Ballet Society, for a subscription audience of one thousand. Two years later, they were asked to become the permanent dance element of New York's City Center, a municipal nonprofit theatrical company of opera and drama. Ballet Society, with George Balanchine as its artistic director, became the New York City Ballet (NYCB). The company gave its first performance on October 11, 1948. That historic program included two pure dance masterpieces, *Concerto Barocco* and *Symphony in C* (1947), to music by Georges Bizet, as well as *Orpheus* (1948), a dramatic retelling of the ancient myth about the Greek musician who descends into the Underworld to search for his wife, Eurydice. Balanchine had commissioned *Orpheus*'s score from Stravinsky and the surrealistic sets and costumes from sculptor Isamu Noguchi. That October evening marked the beginning of an illustrious American company.

## Chapter 28

# Ballet to Broadway and Back Again

During the 1940s, two American choreographers, Agnes de Mille and Jerome Robbins, first received recognition for their uniquely American ballets. Both choreographers enjoyed long careers that have gone from classical ballet to the Broadway stage and back again.

Agnes de Mille (1905–1993) was born in New York City. Her father, William, was a successful playwright, and her mother, Anna, had a strong interest in art, music, and literature. Agnes's uncle, Cecil B. DeMille, was a Hollywood mogul, the most famous movie producer and director of his day.

De Mille said she knew she wanted to be a dancer when she was five years old, but her parents would not let her take lessons. Her father thought that female dancers looked too much like acrobats and were neither ladylike or intelligent. Her mother, while sympathetic to her daughter's desire, felt that formal lessons would spoil her "natural gifts." Like other young girls of her generation, Agnes, then twelve, was taken to see the great Pavlova. The experience, she later said, not only left her speechless but "burned in a single afternoon a path over which I could never retrace my steps." Two years later, her parents relented on lessons, but only because a doctor told them that dancing would strengthen her sister's feet. In the de Mille family, both sisters were always treated exactly alike, so Agnes finally got her chance to study dance at the age of fourteen. She continued her lessons throughout her teenage years (although she was never allowed to practice more than forty-five minutes a day), but thinking that she would never be a professional dancer, she enrolled at UCLA and graduated with honors.

All the while, however, her greatest desire was to dance. After graduating, she spent the next several years auditioning unsuccessfully for Broadway shows and creating choreographic character sketches — such as a dancer suffering from stage fright and a young girl traveling west on a covered wagon — showing her skill for pantomime and comedy. Although her infrequent dance recitals were enthusiastically received, she could not make a living with her art. The 1930s were a decade of hard work but very little success for the young dancer. A loan from her sister enabled her to go to London, where she studied with Marie Rambert, danced with Antony Tudor, and presented recitals of her work that reflected her American roots. After a year, at the request of her uncle, she returned to California to choreograph the dances for his epic film *Cleopatra*. Unfortunately he hated her work — it wasn't lurid enough — and she was fired. Other jobs in Hollywood and on Broadway proved equally unsuccessful.

In 1942, de Mille, thirty-seven, was about to turn her back on the world of dance she loved so much when she auditioned for the chance to create and star in a ballet for the Ballet Russe de Monte Carlo. It had been less than a year since America had entered World War II, and the company wanted to add the novelty of an American ballet to their repertoire. They had already commissioned music for the piece from American composer Aaron Copland. The company selected de Mille as the work's choreographer and principal dancer. The result, *Rodeo: The Courting at Burnt Ranch*, was a landmark work. Set in the American Southwest, it captured the lives of real people doing real things.

The story of *Rodeo* is simple and uniquely American — an awkward, tomboyish cowgirl learns how to get her man, winning the heart of the handsome Champion Roper at the Saturday night barn dance. De Mille devised the scenario working closely with Copland, who filled his score with snatches of familiar cowboy songs and folk tunes. Using ordinary, everyday gestures and stylized movements, she devised steps that made the classically trained dancers look like bowlegged ranch hands riding horseback and lassoing steers. De Mille once said that "ballet is only formalized and dramatized folk dancing," and one of the high points of *Rodeo* is a foot-stomping, hand-clapping square dance. The ballet, and de Mille's dancing in the lead role, were a sensation. There were twenty-two curtain calls at the premiere, and among the many bouquets showered on her was one created from ears of corn tied in ribbons of red, white, and blue. One reviewer called *Rodeo* "as refreshing and as American as Mark Twain." Agnes de Mille was finally a star, and the lights of Broadway beckoned.

Richard Rodgers and Oscar Hammerstein were working on a new show, *Oklahoma!* (1943), with an American theme and setting, and they knew de Mille would be the perfect choice for its choreographer. The dances she created for this love story set against the background of feuding farmers and cowhands in the Oklahoma Territory changed the direction of musical theater.

With the exception of Balanchine's pioneering work, ballet had been used in musicals only as a diverting filler before Agnes de Mille choreographed *Oklahoma!* Instead of the usual lavish chorus-line production numbers that stopped the action, de Mille's dances were totally integrated into the story. They were related to the plot, commented and expanded on the action, and illustrated the emotions of the characters. They incorporated American folk themes. In her work for the musical stage, de Mille was able to portray sentiments that reflected America's hopes and fears. A year after *Oklahoma!* she choreographed a somber and moving ballet about soldiers returning home to their wives for a show called *Bloomer Girl*. Although it was

Agnes de Mille as the Cowgirl in her 1942 ballet, *Rodeo.*

set during the Civil War, the ballet spoke powerfully and directly to the contemporary war-weary audience.

For the next seventeen years, de Mille choreographed a number of Broadway shows that became classics of the American stage, including *Brigadoon* and *Carousel.* She also created works for American Ballet Theatre, including *Fall River Legend* (1948), a dance-drama based on the notorious nineteenth-century trial of Lizzie Borden, accused of murdering her father and stepmother. Eventually confined to a wheelchair, de Mille continued to choreograph ballets

— *The Informer* in 1988, *The Other* in 1992. In all her work — ballet and theatrical — she fused classical steps and folk material into a stylized realism of dramatic detail and keenly observed natural gesture.

Agnes de Mille was a spokesperson for the arts in America. She helped establish the National Endowment for the Arts and in an effort to preserve American dance, founded the Heritage Dance Theater at the North Carolina School of the Arts. She was also a prolific and eloquent writer; her thirteen books include gracious, witty memoirs and highly respected works on dance.

Jerome Robbins, considered by many to be the greatest American-born ballet choreographer, was born in 1918 and grew up in New York City, the son of immigrant parents. Like Agnes de Mille, he made his name on both the Broadway and ballet stages. His works capture the spirit of the American character and the rhythm of American life; many reflect his urban upbringing. A Robbins ballet displays theatrical showmanship and emotional intensity, combining influences from the worlds of modern dance, jazz, Broadway, folk dancing, and the ballroom, as well as George Balanchine's neoclassicism.

Robbins became interested in theater and dance through his older sister, a modern dancer. As a teenager, he studied Spanish, Oriental, and interpretive dance as well as ballet and took lessons in drama, voice, piano, and the violin. Like the de Milles, his parents thought that dancing was not a proper career, so he attended New York University with the idea of becoming a chemist. When there was no money for a second term, he first got a job for fifteen dollars a week as an actor and dancer at the Yiddish Arts Theater, where he was also allowed to choreograph some small pieces, and then as a chorus boy in several Broadway musicals.

Robbins joined American Ballet Theatre in 1940, their first season, as a member of the corps de ballet. Within a year, he was a soloist — an outstanding character dancer doing principal roles in ballets by Fokine, Tudor, Massine, and de Mille. In 1944, when he was twenty-six, Jerome Robbins got his big break as a choreographer. And like de Mille with *Rodeo*, it was with a ballet that was distinctly American and completely different from the typical Russian-style ballets of the day. *Fancy Free* made Robbins a star overnight. When the ballet premiered, Americans had been fighting in World War II for over two and a half years. Robbins's one-act ballet of real-life contemporary America features three young sailors on shore leave in New York City on a warm summer night and shows what happens when they meet two girls. Robbins, who danced the lead sailor, seamlessly melded classical ballet technique with relaxed natural gestures — the sailors chew gum, clown around boisterously, and do versions of 1940s jazz and ballroom dances. The choreography is athletic, with pull-out-the-stops leaps and turns, and it also has a romantic pas de deux. The score, by Leonard Bernstein, then also twenty-six years old, is jazzy and humorous, filled with energy and youthful zest.

*Fancy Free* was a smash — its innocence and gaiety were just the right antidote for audiences weary of war. The ballet was performed ninety-nine times that year and then was expanded by Robbins and Bernstein into an equally popular Broadway musical called *On the Town*. A few years later it was turned into a movie; the ballet itself is still in the active repertoire. Jerome Robbins's long and successful dual career as a choreographer for both ballet and Broadway was launched.

Between 1944 and 1964, Robbins was the choreographer or director-choreographer for sixteen Broadway musicals, including many that are now considered classics: *The King and I* (1951), *Peter Pan* (1954), *Gypsy* (1959), and *Fiddler on the Roof* (1964). In 1957, Robbins collaborated again with Leonard Bernstein on a modern version of Shakespeare's *Romeo and Juliet* — a musical called *West Side*

*Story*. This work fused dancing with drama and was considered a major step forward in musical theater. Agnes de Mille called it *"a ballet d'action* with dialogue." Robbins's highly original, powerfully dramatic choreography ranged from dynamic Latin-flavored dances to a lyric dream ballet to tension-filled fight scenes.

Even while he was working on Broadway, Robbins continued his association with classical ballet. Between 1949 and 1956, he worked with George Balanchine as associate artistic director of the New York City Ballet. His ballets added another dimension to the repertoire of the fledgling company. In 1958, he formed his own troupe, Ballets: U.S.A., to tour Europe and the United States. He returned to the New York City Ballet eleven years later as ballet master, and until he retired from the company in 1990, he shared the title of ballet-master-in-chief with Peter Martins, the company's current director.

Jerome Robbins has created more than sixty ballets in a wide variety of styles and to a wide variety of music. He has even choreographed a ballet to silence (*Moves*, 1959). One of his popular works is *Interplay* (1945). Performed to a jazzy blues score by Morton Gould, it combines the improvisational quality of teenagers choosing up sides for a contest of virtuoso dancing with athletic gymnastics, purely classical steps, and syncopated popular dance movement. The ballet is breezy and good-natured and even slyly spoofs some of the mannerisms and poses of classical dance. *Afternoon of a Faun* (1953) uses the same Debussy score as Nijinsky's earlier ballet, but the Faun and Nymph are now two self-absorbed dance students and the Greek countryside is now a ballet studio. *Dances at a Gathering* (1969), an outpouring of pure dance to Chopin piano pieces, contains many beautiful and difficult lifts and examples of the inventive partnering that are hallmarks of Robbins's ballets. *The Four Seasons* (1979), to ballet scores from several Verdi operas, is a kaleidoscopic trip around the calendar.

In 1983, Robbins choreographed *Glass Pieces*, a ballet to three works by Philip Glass (born in 1937), a leading Minimalist composer. Like its score, the choreography for *Glass Pieces* is based on pulsating repetitive phrases and movements. One reviewer called the ballet "a picture of our systematized times — the electronic age, the computer age." In contrast, *Ives, Songs* (1988) is a look back at life in early twentieth-century America. The ballet, one of his most recent, is set to eighteen songs by innovative New England composer Charles Ives (1874–1954).

*Chapter 29*

# And Now a Home

The early years of the New York City Ballet were not completely successful. Popular and critical reception was sometimes cool to Balanchine's pure-dance ballets with simple staging and costuming. The American dance public was used to seeing the nineteenth-century classics, the psychological dance-dramas of Antony Tudor, or Americana ballets such as de Mille's *Rodeo* or Loring's *Billy the Kid*. An audience had to be built up for the Balanchine repertoire. By the end of the 1950s, Balanchine and Kirstein had done just that. New York City was on its way to becoming the art and cultural capital of the world. There was a freshness and excitement about American dance that could not be matched in Europe.

This was a period of great creativity for Balanchine. He choreographed a new version of Stravinsky's *Firebird* (1949) as well as a two-act *Nutcracker* (1954), the company's first evening-length ballet. He created plotless, pure-dance ballets to the music of Mozart (*Divertimento #15*, 1956) and Tchaikovsky (*Allegro Brillante*, 1956) and to the strange atonal compositions of Austrian Anton von Webern (*Episodes*, 1959). In *Square Dance* (1957), set to eighteenth-century Baroque music by Antonio Vivaldi and Arcangelo Corelli, Balanchine joined American folk dance with classical ballet. The original version of this ballet even had a well-known square dance caller on stage, shouting out the steps. *Square Dance* was not the only work that reflected Balanchine's admiration for the popular culture of his adopted home. The choreographer, who loved TV westerns and often wore silver Indian bracelets and dressed in blue jeans and cowboy shirts, created works using classical ballet steps but danced to unballetic American music. Hershy Kay's score for *Western Symphony* (1954) is based on melodies from a dozen familiar American folk songs, and the dancers are costumed as cowboys and dance hall girls. *Stars and Stripes* (1958) is danced to John Philip Sousa marches.

Balanchine also loved the waltz. In the eerie and macabre *La Valse* (1951), to music by Maurice Ravel, Death comes to claim a young woman at her first ball. In *Liebeslieder Walzer*, created nine years later, four couples waltz the evening away at a fashionable party in nineteenth-century Vienna, to the vocal accompaniment of *lieder*, or songs, by Johannes Brahms. Balanchine's grandest ballet to waltz music is *Vienna Waltzes* (1977), to the music of Johann Strauss Jr., Franz Lehár, and Richard Strauss. In its closing section, sixty dancers — the women in sophisticated white satin gowns, the men in white ties and black tailcoats — swirl in dizzying unison across the floor of a silvery mirrored ballroom.

In 1964, the New York City Ballet moved to its current home, the New York State Theater in Lincoln Center, the newly built arts complex on Manhattan's Upper West Side. The stage at the State Theater, designed with Balanchine's help, was the first in the United States created specifically for dance. For their new home, Balanchine created *Jewels* (1967), the first evening-length abstract, or storyless, ballet. Each of its three acts, *Emeralds*, *Rubies*, and *Diamonds*, is danced in different styles representing three major periods in ballet history. *Emeralds*, the dreamlike opening section to music by French composer Gabriel Fauré, has the softness and mystery of a nineteenth-century Romantic ballet. *Rubies*, set to Stravinsky's Capriccio for Piano and Orchestra, is twentieth-century America — crackling sharp syncopations and prancing energy. The concluding section, *Diamonds*, to Tchaikovsky's Symphony #3, displays all the grandeur, opulence, and regal formality of Petipa and St. Petersburg's Imperial Theatre.

During the 1950s and 1960s, Balanchine continued to develop and refine his neoclassical style. To the academic purity and precision of the Petipa tradition, he added the vitality, speed, energy, and athletic prowess of his new country, giving classical ballet a jazzy American flavor. Balanchine wanted his dancers to "attack" the steps, filling them with such energy that, as one Balanchine ballerina put it, "you can almost see the muscles pushing away the molecules of the air." Lincoln Kirstein said this extroverted style sprang "from our own training and environment"; it was "bred from basketball courts, track and swimming meets, and junior proms. . . . It is frank, open, fresh and friendly. . . . We almost invite [our audiences] to dance with us."

## The Balanchine-Stravinsky Collaboration

Choreographer George Balanchine and composer Igor Stravinsky were two artistic geniuses of the twentieth century. Their work together is one of the great collaborations in ballet history.

Music was the starting point of all Balanchine's ballets. A talented pianist, he sometimes studied a score for ten years, picking it apart note by note, before creating choreography to it. "I couldn't move without a reason," he said, "and the reason is the music."

The two men shared the view that their respective art forms should express balance and harmony. For Stravinsky, music was "order, measure, proportion . . . all those principles that oppose disorder." This was Stravinsky defining music, but it could as easily have been Balanchine defining ballet.

COSTAS

The Balanchine-Stravinsky collaboration in
*Violin Concerto* (1972) illustrates the jazzy,
supercharged, sharp-edged side of the
choreographer's neoclassical style.

Balanchine and Stravinsky were both innovative artists who took
apart the vocabulary or building blocks of their art and reassembled
them in new ways. Over a period of forty-three years, they worked
together on more than thirty ballets, including such masterpieces as
*Apollo* (1928), *Orpheus* (1948), *Violin Concerto* (1972), and *Symphony in
Three Movements* (1972).

In the 1950s, the style of both the composer and choreographer
became sparer, more economical and angular. Stravinsky was beginning
to explore a twelve-tone, not the usual ten-tone, musical scale;
Balanchine was attempting to stretch classical technique even further. In
1957, they collaborated on *Agon* (Greek for contest), a ballet in twelve
movements using twelve dancers, which visualized the complex and
changing rhythms of Stravinsky's twelve-tone serial score. Stravinsky

based the music on a dozen old French melodies. Balanchine, taking as
his starting point a seventeenth-century French manual describing gal-
liards, sarabands, and branles, made these old court dances as contemporary as the music. As in all Balanchine ballets to Stravinsky scores,
*Agon* is punctuated with quirky steps and intricate movements. Although
*Agon* lasts only twenty minutes, it is so densely packed with movement
that it contains more steps than ballets four times as long. Balanchine
called it a "construction in space" and once compared it to an IBM computer. It is ballet that is perfectly in sync with the tension-filled, high-
speed, high-tech second half of the twentieth century.

## Chapter 30

# A Dance Explosion

During the 1960s and 1970s, the popularity of all kinds of theatrical dance, especially ballet, grew enormously throughout the United States, Canada, and Europe. Large companies such as the New York City Ballet and ABT continued to have successful seasons. Regional ballet companies were being founded in greater numbers, and smaller touring companies were bringing ballet to all areas of the country. Rudolf Nureyev's thrilling appearances around the world contributed to this dance explosion. Then in 1970, the great Soviet ballerina Natalia Makarova defected, followed four years later by Mikhail Baryshnikov, another electrifying Russian danseur who immediately captured the public's imagination. As during the Romantic era, ballet dancers made news and were idolized by the public.

Mikhail Baryshnikov, born in 1948, was the Kirov's youngest principal dancer when he defected from a Soviet company touring Canada. The artistic horizons within his homeland were too limited, he said. He wanted to be able to choose his repertoire, work with different choreographers, and experiment with new styles. Baryshnikov's dancing overwhelmed Western audiences. Newspapers called him "a phenomenon," "a talent so prodigious that it may only be described in superlatives." Like Nureyev, Baryshnikov helped popularize ballet, especially in the United States, which became his new home. He joined ABT (forming a celebrated partnership with fiery, outspoken ballerina Gelsey Kirkland), danced briefly with Balanchine's company, then rejoined American Ballet Theatre, eventually becoming its artistic director for nine years. Baryshnikov starred in several TV specials and in motion pictures. In films such as *The Turning Point* and *White Nights*, he played the true-to-life role of a Russian dancer with an infectious smile and a bravura technique.

COSTAS

Suzanne Farrell and her longtime partner, Peter Martins, in a ballet created for her, Balanchine's *Diamonds*. The final section of the evening-length *Jewels* (1967), the ballet, to Tchaikovsky's Symphony #3 in D Major, is an example of the other side of Balanchine's neoclassicism — its regal grandeur.

The dance explosion of the 1960s and 1970s may have been fueled in part by international stars such as Nureyev, Makarova, and Baryshnikov, but the period also saw the emergence of a number of wonderful American-born dancers.

One of the greatest ballerinas of her generation was a young dancer who joined the New York City Ballet in 1961, when she was just sixteen years old. Suzanne Farrell was born Roberta Sue Ficker in Cincinnati in 1945. She picked her new name out of the Manhattan phone book because "it sounded elegant." On her fifteenth birthday she auditioned for the School of American Ballet and was awarded a full scholarship. As a child she had daydreamed about dancing with her idol, Jacques d'Amboise, then one of the company's leading danseurs. A few years later, her daydream was a reality. Until her retirement in 1988, she was considered the finest interpreter of both aspects of George Balanchine's style — his regal homages to the classical Petipa tradition as well as the sharp-edged ballets to Stravinsky and other modern composers. Suzanne Farrell was the choreographer's quintessential muse. He called her "an alabaster princess" and "the greatest dancer I ever saw," and he created twenty-three roles for her. Farrell was a ballerina of great stage mystery, musical sensitivity, and bold spontaneity. Her physical daring was legendary. She thrilled audiences with the way she could move unpredictably and dramatically from off-balance poses and positions and with the way she would challenge her partners in their pas de deux. She was known for her speed, her dramatic ability, and her passion and abandon. According to Jacques d'Amboise, she often danced "like she was possessed of a demon."

Among the final generation of dancers singled out by Balanchine are two of today's most celebrated ballerinas: Kyra Nichols and Darci Kistler. Nichols (born in 1958) is from Berkeley, California, and began studying dance at the age of four with her mother, a former member of the New York City Ballet. A star pupil at SAB in her early teens,

Nichols became a principal dancer at the age of twenty-one. A tall, powerful presence on stage, she radiates uncommon self-assurance, dancing the most technically difficult steps with ease, grace, and classical purity.

Kistler, born in Riverside, California, in 1964, was the last young dancer Balanchine personally selected for his company. The only girl in a family that included four athletic older brothers, she took her first ballet lesson at the age of six after being enthralled by a performance of *The Sleeping Beauty* starring Fonteyn and Nureyev. She went to New York to study at SAB when she was fourteen and was quickly noticed by Balanchine. The fair-haired, sports-loving dancer joined NYCB in 1980, at age sixteen, and was immediately given leading roles. Two years later, she was made a principal, the company's youngest.

Over the years, many noted danseurs have also been members of the New York City Ballet, including several men trained by the Royal Danish Ballet. From the late 1960s to the mid–1970s, however, two of the company's most popular male dancers were Americans, former SAB students with athletic street-smart styles: Jacques d'Amboise (born in 1934) and Edward Villella (born in 1936). While still a principal dancer, d'Amboise founded the National Dance Institute, an organization that gives free dance training to public school children, resulting in yearly performances directed and choreographed by professionals.

Edward Villella, who was born in Queens, New York, was one of America's greatest male dancers. He was noted for his exuberant energy and theatricality — his remarkable leaps and explosive, athletic style. As a young boy, Villella had been dragged to his sister's dance lessons at the School of American Ballet (to keep him out of trouble, said his mother). One day he participated in a class and was hooked. He stopped going to SAB when he was fifteen, however, because his parents wanted him to get a college education, to have a

George Balanchine and Edward Villella rehearsing, 1972.

"real" career. He attended New York Maritime College (where he was welterweight boxing champion) for four years. But while he was getting his degree in marine transportation, he was also keeping in shape by practicing a daily ballet class in secret. He graduated in 1957 and was immediately asked to join the New York City Ballet. His first solo role was in Jerome Robbins's *Afternoon of a Faun*. Later, the choreographer told Villella that the young dancer had been the inspiration for the ballet. Years before, Robbins had seen SAB's star pupil alone in a studio, lying on the floor. Villella was silhouetted in a shaft of sunlight, stretching unself-consciously; that scene became the ballet's opening movement. During his twenty-two-year career,

Villella danced important roles in the Balanchine repertoire, including the principal roles in *Prodigal Son* and *Rubies*. After retiring from NYCB, he became director of the Miami City Ballet.

Villella's dancing partner for many years was Patricia McBride, a vivacious ballerina of speed, lyricism, and wit who worked with Balanchine longer than any other ballerina. She was born in Teaneck, New Jersey, in 1943 and became a principal dancer before she was eighteen. McBride, who retired from the stage in 1989, had a career that lasted almost thirty years.

American ballerinas often have long careers. Cynthia Gregory, born in Los Angeles in 1946, danced for more than three decades. In 1965, after four years with the San Francisco Ballet, she joined American Ballet Theatre. The company had originally turned her down because she was too tall — on pointe, she stood five-foot-ten. But they could not ignore her dazzling technique and versatility. Gregory has excelled in Romantic and classical roles *(Giselle, La Sylphide, Swan Lake, The Sleeping Beauty, Coppélia)*, as well as in the dramatic ballets of Tudor, de Mille, and MacMillan.

## All Across the Continent

Nearly every large city in the United States and Canada has a professional ballet company. The oldest companies in the U.S. are the San Francisco Ballet (1933) and the Atlanta Ballet (1944). The Pennsylvania Ballet was founded in 1962 by teacher Barbara Weisberger, who had been the first child accepted by George Balanchine into the School of American Ballet. The Boston Ballet was founded in 1964 by a Balanchine protégée, E. Virginia Williams; since 1985 the troupe has been run by Bruce Marks.

Several other city or regional companies are directed by former New York City Ballet dancers: the Fort Worth Ballet (Paul Meija, husband of Suzanne Farrell), Ballet Chicago (Daniel Duell), Seattle's Pacific Northwest Ballet (husband and wife Kent Stowell and Francia Russell), the Pittsburgh Ballet Theater (Patricia Wilde), the Atlanta Ballet (Robert Barnett), the State Ballet of Missouri (Todd Bolender), and the Miami City Ballet (Edward Villella).

There are also professional ballet companies in Dallas; Dayton; Fresno; Hartford; Indianapolis; Louisville; Milwaukee; Sacramento; Toledo; Tulsa; Washington, D.C.; and on Long Island (the Eglevsky Ballet). Several cities share companies: the Cincinnati Ballet has seasons in Knoxville and New Orleans, for example, and the Cleveland Ballet also performs as the San Jose Ballet. State companies include the Alabama Ballet, the Ohio Ballet, the State Ballet of Rhode Island, and Ballet West (Utah).

Canada's largest classical company, the National Ballet of Canada (headquartered in Toronto), was founded in 1951 by a de Valois–trained dancer who had also studied with Marie Rambert. Les Grands Ballets Canadiens of Montreal was originally founded in 1952 as a company to present ballet on local television; two years later they began stage performances. Other Canadian companies include the Royal Winnipeg Ballet, started as an amateur ballet club in 1939 and granted a royal charter in 1953, as well as the Alberta Ballet, the Calgary City Ballet, the Ottowa Ballet, and Ballet British Columbia, based in Vancouver.

## Chapter 31

# "Responsive to Our Times"

Like all art forms, ballet reflects the surrounding society. The 1960s and 1970s were turbulent years in the United States. Three charismatic leaders — John F. Kennedy, Martin Luther King Jr., and Robert F. Kennedy — were assassinated. There was student unrest, urban riots, and numerous massive demonstrations for civil rights and against America's participation in the Vietnam War. It was a time of social and political upheaval that featured hippies and the counter-culture, Watergate, the resignation of President Richard Nixon, the birth of the women's movement, the environmental movement, and the sexual revolution. These concerns were echoed in the dance world. There were psychedelic ballets and ballets danced to rock music and electronic scores. There were ballets that portrayed alien-ation and violence, and others that celebrated African rituals and flower children. There were anti-war ballets and ballets in which the dancers ended up nude.

The repertoire of the Joffrey Ballet, founded in 1956, often reflected the country's concerns. During the 1960s and 1970s, this national touring company became known for its youthful zest and energetic, explosive style. The Joffrey Ballet was founded by two dancer-choreographers, Seattle-born Robert Joffrey (1930–1988) and Gerald Arpino (born in 1928), from Staten Island, New York. The original company consisted of six dancers. Joffrey's desire was "a company that happened out of here, out of America." In a borrowed station wagon, the dancers (who also had to take care of the lights, props, costumes, and sometimes the music) began a series of one-night stands around rural America. Since then the Joffrey Ballet has performed in more than four hundred U.S. cities and has also toured the Near, Far, and Middle East, Europe, and Russia.

Joffrey and Arpino envisioned a company of American dancers that "would be responsive to our times," and one of Robert Joffrey's best known choreographic efforts was the first ballet ever to make the cover of *Time* magazine. *Astarte* (1967), an encounter between a modern-day Love Goddess and an Everyman, who steps out of the audience to join her onstage (stripping off his clothes on the way), was a powerful reflection of the psychedelic sixties. The multimedia ballet combined dance, film, strobe lights, and rock music. The spirit of the times was also captured in two ballets by Gerald Arpino: *The Clowns* (1968), a parable about survival after a nuclear holocaust, and *Trinity* (1969), a celebration of youth and the peace movement. In 1973, the Joffrey commissioned Twyla Tharp's *Deuce Coupe*, a confrontation between ballet and rock and roll that featured music by the Beach Boys and scenery created on the spot each performance by graffiti artists. The company was also the first classical troupe to give a commission to a modern dance choreographer. In 1962, Joffrey asked Alvin Ailey, a young choreographer whose work reflected his African-American heritage, to do a piece for the group. Today, the company's repertoire ranges from Frederick Ashton to Paul Taylor and includes works by Jiří Kylián, head of the Netherlands Dance Theater, by Canadian choreographer James Kudelka, and by American Laura Dean. Their repertoire also features two evening-length works based on Shakespeare plays — *Romeo and Juliet* and *The Taming of the Shrew* — created by John Cranko, a talented British choreographer who died in 1973 at the age of forty-six. Cranko was noted for dramatic and comic ballets that mixed technical virtuosity with acting ability and for his theatrical, athletic, yet classical style, full of individual characterizations and inventive, difficult lifts and steps. The Joffrey Ballet has also been instrumental in reviving and restoring historically important lost ballets, especially those of the Diaghilev era.

Another company born during this turbulent period was the Dance Theatre of Harlem, founded in 1969 by Arthur Mitchell (born in 1934). A principal dancer with the New York City Ballet for eleven years, he had been the first African-American to be a permanent member of a major classical ballet company. Mitchell was moved by the assassination of Martin Luther King Jr. "to introduce young people, particularly those who were economically and culturally disadvantaged, to the beauty and discipline of dance." The Dance Theatre of Harlem, originally all African-American but now a multi-racial company, gave its first performance in 1971. Its school, begun in the basement of a Harlem church, now has several hundred students from all over the country. The company's repertoire is classical, ethnic, and contemporary, and includes works by Fokine, Balanchine, de Mille, Smuin, Glen Tetley, and African-American modern dance choreographers Ailey, Garth Fagan, and Geoffrey Holder. The company has also staged a Creole *Giselle,* set in the free black society that existed in the Louisiana bayous before the Civil War.

New York City is also the home to Feld Ballets/NY, a youthful ensemble founded in 1974 by a former ABT dancer, Eliot Feld (born in 1943). He choreographed his first ballets in 1967 — the lyrical *Harbinger,* to music by Prokofiev, and *At Midnight,* a moody, haunting work to Gustav Mahler. His vision of contemporary American ballet is that it ought to freely incorporate all kinds of movement yet remain true to classical elegance. Feld is also the founder of the New Ballet School, which has a program to provide tuition-free, professional ballet training to talented New York City schoolchildren. Several dancers in his company have joined the group directly from the school.

## Behind the Scenes

A ballet stage is a frenetic place, even before the curtain rises and the performance begins. During the day, while the dancers are rehearsing, the stage crew and personnel are preparing and testing the lights and scenery and checking the props. Stagehands are hanging the backdrops on metal pipes that will be raised and lowered from the flies, the area high above the stage. Electricians are adjusting the gels, the sheets of hard plastic put in front of the lights to change their color. At the back of the theater, high up near the ceiling, other electricians are testing the follow spots, the bright spotlights that will highlight individual dancers on stage. Although all the other stage lighting is computerized, the huge follow spots must be operated manually. Each follow spot may require up to four operators, who must all be familiar with the ballets. By 7:00 p.m., everything is in place. The stage is given a final mopping so there is nothing on the floor that might trip the dancers.

Half an hour before the performance is scheduled to begin, the production stage manager (the backstage "choreographer" in charge of coordinating all the activity before and during a performance) announces over the loudspeaker, "Ladies and gentlemen, thirty minutes." The musicians can now begin entering the orchestra pit. Shortly before the performance is scheduled to start, the production stage manager will announce "Opening preset," the cue, or direction, for the lighting director to bring up the lights for the first ballet. Then comes the five-minute warning call for the dancers, followed a few minutes later by "On stage."

When the production stage manager is satisfied that everything is ready, he or she issues the "House lights down" call, gives the conductor the cue to enter the orchestra pit, and announces a last call for the

dancers: "Places, please." Only when the manager is satisfied that everyone and everything is in its proper place can that night's magic begin to
unfold: "Curtain up."

# Chapter 32
# The Eighties and Beyond

On April 30, 1983, George Balanchine died in New York City of pneumonia at the age of seventy-nine. He had been suffering for several months from a debilitating neurological illness.

Balanchine had transformed ballet. He not only changed the look of classical dance, but taught people how to look at dance with fresh eyes. Although he often said that he merely "assembled" ballets and that choreography was just a skill like cooking or a craft like cabinet-making, Balanchine almost single-handedly raised American ballet into a first-class art form. During his sixty-year career, he had created more than 350 works, not only for the ballet stage but for opera, musical theater, film, and television as well.

After Balanchine's death, choreographer Jerome Robbins and former principal dancer Peter Martins took over running the New York City Ballet, sharing the title of ballet-master-in-chief. When Robbins retired in 1990, Martins became sole ballet-master-in-chief.

Peter Martins (born in 1946), a native of Copenhagen, trained at the Royal Danish Ballet School and became a principal dancer with their company when he was twenty-one. His relationship with the New York City Ballet began in the summer of 1967. Balanchine's company was participating in the Edinburgh Festival when Jacques d'Amboise, scheduled to dance *Apollo* with Suzanne Farrell, was injured. Martins, the only dancer in Europe at the time who knew the role, was asked to fill in. For the next three years, he guested with the

American company, finally joining them permanently as a principal in 1970. For the next thirteen years, until he stopped dancing in 1983, the handsome, blond, six-foot-two danseur thrilled American audiences with his charismatic stage presence, aristocratic elegance, grace, strength, musicality, and flawless partnering.

Martins began his choreographic career while still a dancer. His first ballet, *Calcium Light Night* (1977), was choreographed to the unconventional music of Charles Ives. In this and the more than fifty ballets he has since made, he has worked within the Balanchine style, exploring the art of partnering and further developing and extending the role of male dancers. Like his predecessor, Martins has choreographed ballets to the radiant melodies of Tchaikovsky and the jazzy rhythms of Stravinsky. Martins, who once considered becoming an architect, has also shown an affinity for the cool harmony, structure, and balance of Baroque music, as well as the hot, driving energy of contemporary American composers such as Michael Torke, John Adams, and Wynton Marsalis.

## A Dancer's Day

A professional ballet dancer's day is full and long. During performing seasons, dancers may work six days a week for many weeks on end.

| | |
|---|---|
| 7:00–10:00 A.M. | Rise and Shine |
| | Breakfast, feed the cat, walk the dog, do the laundry, shop for groceries, clean the house. |
| 10:30 A.M.–noon | Company Class |
| 12:30–6:00 P.M. | Rehearsals |
| | (On weekends, there might also be matinee performances.) |

| | |
|---|---|
| 6:00–8:00 P.M. | Dinner Break |
| | A spare meal and preparation for the |
| | evening performance |
| 8:00–10:30 P.M. | On Stage |
| 11:00 P.M. | Home to Bed |

Dressed in ragtag T-shirts, old leotards, torn tights, and bulky leg warmers, the dancers entering the studio for their morning company class look nothing like the elegant beings that will perform on stage later that night. For an hour and a half, they go through warm-up exercises — barre and center work to loosen their joints and stretch the muscles. At the barre, the dancers begin by doing pliés. They continue with exercises to stretch the feet, develop quick footwork, and promote control. During the second half of the class, the dancers move to the center of the floor to practice combinations of steps and their adagio technique — the slow port de bras, arabesques, and other movements to develop balance and control; then comes allegro work — pirouettes and traveling and jumping steps. The class might end with practicing double, or support, work — partnering and lifts.

In the afternoons, the dancers have many hours of rehearsals, learning new ballets or perfecting ones they already know. They also have to spend time at costume fittings and breaking in their shoes.

After a short break for dinner, the dancers are back at the theater to get ready for that evening's performance. They need to arrange their hair, put on their stage makeup, and check that their shoes are ready to dance in.

When hair and makeup is done and headpieces and tiaras are securely pinned in place, dancers do another round of barre exercises to warm up their muscles. It is then time to get into costume. Principal dancers have their costumes brought to them in their dressing rooms; the male and female corps gets ready in their own large dressing rooms. Dancers need help getting in and out of their costumes. Ballet costumes do not use zippers, which might open, with embarrassing results, during a performance. They are closed with many little hooks and eyes. Each costume has shoulder straps (usually invisible from the audience) and several rows of fasteners, so it can be easily adjusted to fit dancers of different sizes.

A dancer's day is not over until the performance is ended, often close to 11:00 P.M. The last thing a dancer does before leaving the theater is to consult the backstage call sheet, the schedule of the next day's rehearsals.

In the 1980s and 1990s, other dancer-choreographers were also expanding their own visions and styles. One of the most electrifying is Twyla Tharp. Born in 1942, Tharp began her career in 1965 as a controversial modern dance choreographer. Over the years she has created more and more dances using classical technique and vocabulary, blurring the line between modern dance and ballet. Tharp's distinctive style has been described as casual and flippant, loose-jointed and slinky — her dancers shuffle, shimmy, and ripple; they shrug their shoulders and wiggle their heads. Tharp's ballets contain abrupt changes in direction or tempo and unpredictable, unexpected movements that have no apparent preparation. Dancers are sometimes thrown about in hair-raising cartwheels or career wildly across the stage. Although her works may look tossed off and informal, they are meticulously structured, crafted, and rehearsed, and are full of precise, complex footwork. They incorporate everyday gestures as well as steps from social dances, from square dancing to disco. Her dancers may wear ballet slippers or jazz shoes.

Tharp was twenty-three and had been dancing with the Paul Taylor Dance Company for two years when she formed her own troupe, Twyla Tharp and Dancers. She has created over seventy works to a wide variety of music: from popular recordings of Frank Sinatra, Chuck Berry, and Paul Simon to classical pieces by Mozart, Bach, Brahms to traditional American jazz and country music. In *Push Comes to Shove* (1976), made specifically for Mikhail Baryshnikov, Tharp juxtaposes American ragtime and the Baroque strains of Franz Joseph Haydn. In addition to choreographing for American Ballet Theatre, where she was associate artistic director for two years, she has done work for the New York City Ballet, as well as for films and Broadway.

Another contemporary choreographer with a distinctive style is William Forsythe, born in New York City in 1949. Forsythe, who trained with the Joffrey Ballet, has choreographed for the Paris Opera Ballet, the San Francisco Ballet, the New York City Ballet, and other companies around the world. Since 1984, he has been director of Germany's Frankfurt Ballet. Forsythe is noted for energetic, theatrical new wave ballets with themes that often reflect the violence and hostility of popular culture and society and the frustrations of modern-day life and love. He often asks his dancers to break away from the traditional vocabulary of classical ballet — movements that create an improvisational look and mood, off-balance turns and partnering, split-second timing, daggerlike pointe work that slashes the air and jabs the floor, novel port de bras done in unexpected directions and in tempos that do not always correspond to those of the feet. Forsythe says he wants his dancers to take physical and emotional risks on stage. Spoken texts, sounds, and novel lighting, scenery, props, and costumes can play important parts in his ballets. Forsythe sometimes gives his works unusual names like *in the middle, somewhat elevated* (1988) and *Herman Schmerman* (1992). In *Behind the China Dogs* (1988), the score is a high-tech collage of the recordings of jazz trumpeter Louis Armstrong, a von Webern string quartet, barking dogs, and a rolling bowling ball.

The work of Mark Morris, the flamboyant, impish "bad boy" of postmodern dance, also blends ballet and modern dance techniques. Born in Seattle in 1956, Morris, who is both a fine dancer and a prolific dance maker, is known for works that are innovative, musical, idiosyncratic, and occasionally outrageous. Morris studied both ballet and folk dance, and he has an affinity for the Baroque music of Bach and Vivaldi. He often uses narrative and abstract dance in the same piece. One of his trademarks is the equality of the sexes on stage.

Graduating students from the School of American Ballet, one of the world's leading ballet academies.

Women may partner women, men may partner men, and women sometimes do the lifting and carrying. Morris has been known to dance female roles himself, because, he says, "they are the best parts." Many of the dancers in his own company look like ordinary people and have a variety of body types — tall or short, heavy or thin.

Ballet, born over four hundred years ago at a royal French court, remains a popular entertainment today, enjoyed by millions of people through live performances and on videos, television, and film. It has come a long way from the days when refined and elegant ladies and gentlemen, resplendent in their court finery, paraded and promenaded in stately measure around vast palace halls. The art has traveled many miles and many years, from France and Italy to Russia, England, and America, to countries all around the world. Its traditions have survived the tumultuous upheavals of wars and revolutions and the constant changes in cultural tastes and opinions. And through it all, its magical spell has remained the same. As it enters its fifth century, ballet — that ever-enduring, ever-evolving art of beauty, romance, excitement, and daring — continues to enchant, to carry audiences away on wings of joy.

# Coda

To dance . . . is to step out on the
great stages of the world . . . a
carpet of music spread under you
each night, to flash and soar . . . to
ride violins and trumpets . . . to
feel the magic work.

— Agnes de Mille
From *To a Young Dancer*

# Glossary

*adagio* (ah-DAH-gee-oh): one of the few Italian ballet terms; it refers to slow, sustained movements and graceful poses or to the class exercises done to perfect balance and line.

*allegro* (ah-LEH-groh): another Italian word, a musical term applied to quick, lively steps; all steps done in the air — jumps, turns, entrechats — are allegro movements.

*arabesque* (ar-uh-BESK): one of the basic poses in ballet; standing on one foot with the other leg extended straight behind the body, the foot pointed, the dancer creates a long, flowing line from fingertips to toes.

*ballet* (ba-LAY): from the Italian *ballare*, to dance, and *balleto*, little dance; the theatrical art form that through movement and music tells a story without words or conveys moods or emotions.

*ballet d'action* (ba-LAY dak-SYAWn): a ballet with a story or plot, such as *Giselle*, for example.

*ballon* (bah-LOHn): lightness or bounciness; the ability to pause a little at the height of a jump and then land softly.

*barre* (bahr): the wooden handrail that dancers use as a support during their warm-up exercises.

*battement* (baht-MAHn): an extension of the leg followed by a beating action of the extended foot against the supporting leg.

*batterie* (baht-REE): any movement in which the feet beat together or one foot beats against the other.

*bourrée* (boo-RAY): small, quick, even steps, usually done on pointe, that give the impression of gliding or skimming across the floor.

*cabriole* (KA-bree-ohl): a high, goatlike leap.

*choreography* (kor-ee-AW-gruh-fee): from the Greek for dance and writing, the steps and patterns of a ballet or dance composition.

*classical:* the term applied to the academic form of ballet, the *ballet d'école*, and its vocabulary of steps and movements. The term does not refer to subject matter: Romantic ballets like *Giselle* are classical, as are many contemporary abstract, or plotless, works. The term *classical Russian ballet* refers to the ballets produced in imperial Russia during the last thirty years of the nineteenth century.

*corps de ballet* (kor duh ba-LAY): literally "the body of the ballet"; the dancers who do not appear as soloists but as a large group or ensemble, usually doing the same steps.

*danseur noble* (dah*n*-SER NAW-bluh): a male dancer who excels in the classical style of ballet.

*développé* (deh-veh-loh-PAY): a smooth and gradual unfolding of one leg (toward the front, side, or back) as it is raised into a bent position, past the ankle as far as the knee of the other leg, then into a straight position away from the body.

*divertissement* (dee-VEHR-tees-MAH*n*): from the French for enjoyment or diversion; a series of short, usually showy dances inserted into a ballet that often bear no relationship to the story but are meant to highlight the talents of the dancers; it also refers to a solo, pas de deux, or other segment from a longer ballet that is presented on its own.

*élancer* (ay-lah*n*-SAY): to dart. One of the seven movements of ballet.

*enchaînement* (ah*n*-shen-MAH*n*): a linking of two or more steps to form a continuous movement; *enchaînements* may form a variation, or solo dance.

*enlèvement* (ahn-lev-MAHn): a step or pose in which one dancer lifts another. Lifts require a split-second collaboration that involves timing, balance, and breathing. Just as her partner is about to lift her, the ballerina must breathe in and push off from the ground. Once she is in the air, the danseur must straighten out his arms and lock his elbows in order to keep her aloft.

*entrechat* (ah*n*-truh-SHAH): literally interweaving; a step, beginning and ending in fifth position, in which the dancer jumps into the air while rapidly crossing the legs before and behind each other.

*entrée* (ah*n*-TRAY): the entrance of a dancer or group of dancers in a divertissement. The term sometimes refers to the divertissement itself.

*étendre* (ay-TAH*n*-druh): to stretch; one of the seven movements of ballet. The adjective, *tendu* (tah*n*-DEW), is often used to describe battements.

*fish dive:* an exciting step in which the ballerina is caught by her partner as she fearlessly swoops, head first, to the floor, her body curved, her legs raised and feet crossed to resemble a fish's tail.

*fouetté* (foo-eh-TAY): a complete spin on one foot during which the ballerina raises and lowers herself on and off pointe while her other leg whips around to give momentum.

*glissade* (glee-SAHD): a gliding or traveling step used to link other steps.

*glisser* (glee-SAY): to glide; one of the seven movements of ballet.

*jeté* (zhuh-TAY): literally "thrown"; a spring or a leap from one foot to the other. The *grand jeté* is a bounding leap forward with legs outstretched.

*leotard* (LEE-uh-tard): a skintight garment covering the torso, usually worn with tights. Named for Jules Léotard, a nineteenth-century French aerialist and gymnast.

*pas d'action* (pah-dahk-SYAWn): a combination of dancing and mime that reveals plot or character; any scene in which the narrative is carried forward by dancing.

*pas de deux* (pah duh duh): a dance for two; a duet.

*pas de trois* (pah duh trwah): a dance for three.

*pirouette* (peer-oo-ET): literally a whirl or spin; a complete turn of the body performed on one foot and usually on pointe.

*plié* (PLEE-ay): a bending of the knees; the basis of all ballet steps; all jumps begin and end with a plié.

*plier* (plee-AY): to bend; one of the seven movements of ballet.

*port de bras* (por duh brah): literally "carriage of the arms"; any of various positions and movements of the arms.

*relevé* (reh-leh-VAY): an elevation of the body, either *sur les pointes* (sewr lay PWENT), on the toes, or *sur les demi-pointes* (sewr lay deh-mee PWENT), on the balls of the feet.

*relever* (reh-leh-VAY): to rise; one of the seven movements of ballet.

*rond de jambe* (rohn duh zhahmb): literally "circle of the leg"; a circular movement of the leg that can be done *à terre* (ah tehr), on the ground, or *en l'air* (ahn lehr), in the air.

*sauter* (soh-TAY): to jump; one of the seven movements of ballet. *Sauté* (soh-TAY) is the adjective applied to a step that is jumped.

*tourner* (toor-NAY): to turn; one of the seven movements of ballet. A *tour en l'air* (toor ahn lehr) is a turn, mostly done by male dancers, in which the dancer rises straight up from fifth position and whips his body into one or more complete revolutions before landing.

*tutu* (TOO-too): the dress worn by a ballerina. It has a fitted bodice and a skirt made up of layers of gathered tulle or net. The Romantic tutu has a long skirt ending below the calf; the classical tutu has a short, stiff circular skirt, attached to ruffled underpants.

# Bibliography

## General Ballet History

Anderson, Jack. *Dance*. New York: Newsweek Books, 1974.

Balanchine, George, and Francis Mason. *Balanchine's Complete Stories of the Great Ballets*. Garden City, New York: Doubleday, 1968.

Bland, Alexander. *A History of Ballet and Dance in the Western World*. New York: Praeger Publishers, 1976.

de Mille, Agnes. *The Book of Dance*. New York: Golden Press, 1963.

Dodd, Craig. *Ballet and Modern Dance*. New York: Elsevier Dutton, 1980.

Fonteyn, Margot. *The Magic of Dance*. New York: Knopf, 1979.

Grant, Gail. *Technical Manual and Dictionary of Classical Ballet*, 2nd revised edition. New York: Dover, 1967.

Guest, Ivor. *Dancer's Heritage: A Short History of Ballet*. London: Dancing Times, 1970.

Kirstein, Lincoln. *Four Centuries of Ballet*. New York: Dover, 1984.

Lawson, Joan. *A History of Ballet and Its Makers*. New York: Pitman, 1964.

———. *The Story of Ballet*. New York: Taplinger, 1976.

Lyntham, Derick. *Ballet Then and Now*. London: Sylvan, 1947.

Moore, Lillian. *Images of the Dance: Historical Treasures of the Dance Collection, 1581–1861*. New York: New York Public Library; Astor, Lenox and Tilden Foundations, 1965.

Selby-Lowndes, Joan. *World Ballet*. New York: Galahad, 1981.

Terry, Walter. *Star Performance: The Stories of the World's Great Ballerinas*. Garden City, New York: Doubleday, 1954.

## Nineteenth-Century Ballet

Blasis, Carlo. *The Code of Terpsichore*. Brooklyn: Dance Horizons, 1976.

Gautier, Théophile. *The Romantic Ballet as Seen by Théophile Gautier*. Translated by Cyril Beaumont. Originally published in 1932. New York: Arno, 1980.

Guest, Ivor. *The Romantic Ballet in Paris*. Princeton: Princeton Book Company, 1966.

Krasovskaya, Vera. *Marius Petipa and The Sleeping Beauty*. New York: Dance Perspectives, 1972.

Roslavleva, Natalia. *Era of the Russian Ballet*. New York: Da Capo, 1979.

Ross-McKenzie, Constance. *How to Mime*. London: Kenyan-Deane, n.d.

Samactson, Dorothy and Joseph. *The Russian Ballet*. New York: Lothrop Lee & Shepard, 1971.

Sorley, Katherine. *Eye on Mime*. New York: Walker, 1969.

Stonimsky, Yuri. *Marius Petipa*. New York: Dance Index, 1947.

Terry, Walter. *Bournonville: The King's Dancing Master*. New York: Dodd Mead, 1979.

## Twentieth-Century Ballet

Aria, Barbara. *Misha: The Mikhail Baryshnikov Story*. New York: St. Martin's, 1989.

Ballets Russes souvenir programs. London and Paris: 1909–1921.

Barnes, Clive. *Nureyev*. New York: Helene Obolensky, 1982.

Beaumont, Cyril. *Vaslav Nijinsky*. New York: Haskel House, 1974.

Bland, Alexander. *Fonteyn and Nureyev*. New York: Times Books, 1979.

Buckle, Richard, in collaboration with John Taras. *George Balanchine, Ballet Master: A Biography*. New York: Random House, 1988.

———. *Nijinsky*. New York: Simon & Schuster, 1971.

Chujoy, Anatole. *The New York City Ballet*. New York: Knopf, 1953.

de Mille, Agnes. *Dance to the Piper and Promenade Home: A Two-Part Autobiography*. New York: Da Capo, 1980.

———. *Speak to Me, Dance with Me*. Boston: Little, Brown, 1973.

Farrell, Suzanne, with Toni Bentley. *Holding On to the Air: An Autobiography*. New York: Summit, 1990.

Kerensky, Oleg. *Anna Pavlova*. New York: Dutton, 1973.

Lieven, Prince Peter. *The Birth of the Ballets Russes*. Translated by L. Zarine. Originally published by George Allen & Unwin, London, 1936. New York: Dover, 1973.

Martins, Peter. *Far from Denmark*. Boston: Little, Brown, 1982.

Maynard, Olga. *The American Ballet*. Philadelphia: Macrae Smith, 1959.

Nijinska, Bronislava. *Bronislava Nijinska: Early Memoirs*. Translated and edited by Irini Nijinska and Jean Rawlinson. New York: Holt, Rinehart, Winston, 1981.

Pavlova, Anna. *Pavlova: Portrait of a Dancer*. Edited by Margot Fonteyn. New York: Viking, 1984.

Percival, John. *The World of Diaghilev*. New York: Dutton, 1971.

Reynolds, Nancy. *Repertory in Review: Forty Years of the New York City Ballet*. New York: Dial, 1977.

Roslavleva, Natalia. *Era of the Russian Ballet*. New York: Da Capo, 1979.

Simmonds, Harvey, editor. *Choreography by George Balanchine: A Catalogue of Works*. New York: Viking, 1984.

Stead, Richard. *Ballets Russes*. Secaucus, New Jersey: Wellfleet, 1989.

Steinberg, Cobbett. *San Francisco Ballet: The First Fifty Years*. San Francisco: San Francisco Ballet Association, 1983.

Stravinsky, Igor. *An Autobiography*. New York: Norton, 1962.

Taper, Bernard. *Balanchine: A Biography*. New York: Times Books, 1984.

Vaughn, David. *Frederick Ashton and His Ballets*. New York: Knopf, 1977.

Villella, Edward, with Larry Kaplan. *Prodigal Son: Dancing for Balanchine in a World of Pain and Magic*. New York: Simon & Schuster, 1992.

Volkov, Solomn. *Balanchine's Tchaikovsky: Interviews with George Balanchine*. Translated by Antonina W. Bouis. New York: Simon & Schuster, 1985.

Young, Percy M. *Stravinsky*. New York: David White, 1969.

# Index